WHY HEBREW
GOES FROM
RIGHT TO LEFT

WHY HEBREW GOES FROM RIGHT TO LEFT

201 Things You Never Knew About Judaism

RABBI RONALD H. ISAACS

KTAV PUBLISHING HOUSE, INC.
Jersey City, New Jersey
2008

Copyright 2008 Ronald H. Isaacs
ISBN 978-1-60280-031-1

Library of Congress Cataloging-in-Publication Data

Isaacs, Ronald H.
Why Hebrew goes from right to left :
201 things you never knew about Judaism /
by Ronald H. Isaacs.

p. cm.

Includes bibliographical references.

ISBN 978-1-60280-031-1

1. Judaism—Miscellanea.
2. Curiosities and wonders.
I. Title. II.
Title: 201 things you never knew about Judaism.
III. Title: Two hundred one things
you never knew about Judaism.

BM45.I755   2008

296—dc22   2008008942

Published by
KTAV Publishing House, Inc.
930 Newark Avenue
Jersey City, NJ 07306
Email: bernie@ktav.com
www.ktav.com
(201) 963–9524
Fax (201) 963–0102

Contents

Chapter 3
UNUSUAL SUPERSTITIONS   33

Chapter 4
DREAMS   41

Chapter 5
DEMONS, SPIRITS, AND EVIL FORCES   47

Introduction

These days, books about Judaism and Jewish life abound. There are informational books about the Jewish life-cycle, Jewish holiday books, books about how to do Jewish ritual, books about synagogue practices, books of Jewish history, and books that cover the whole range of Jewish ethics. The intention of this volume is to present some surprising and fascinating information about Jews and Judaism that you never knew but, I believe, will surely be interested to know.

In American culture in general today, there is increased interest in doing stories and documenting, both in the print and television media, some of the more fascinating persons and places that make up the fabric of American life. As a rabbi I have always enjoyed learning some of the lesser-known things about Judaism and Jewish life, things that are less likely to make it into the print media but nevertheless are fascinating and sometimes, quite frankly, downright wondrous. Over the years I have collected some of the more unusual and unknown curiosities, oddities, surprises, and other bits of information that you will find entertaining and be surprised to learn. I hope that you find your reading of this book both enjoyable and edifying. Perhaps you will want to continue to explore the Jewish heritage using this book as your motivation.

I wish you happy reading, and once again I thank Bernie Scharfstein and Ktav Publishing House for the opportunity to share my findings and research with you.

CHAPTER 1

The Hebrew Language

1. Did you ever wonder why Hebrew is written and read from right to left?

The Hebrew language is an ancient one, likely more than 4,000 years old. Centuries ago, before there was paper or even parchment, anything that was written down was actually chiseled into stone or impressed on a clay tablet. Research has shown that if one is right-handed (as the majority of us are), it is more natural and easier to be precise with the motion of chiseling a language from the right. A modern example might be hammering a nail into a piece of wood. If you are right-handed, you will hold the nail in your left hand and hammer with your right, allowing for more accuracy.

People who are left-handed have a marked disadvantage writing in any language that goes from left to right if they are writing with a pen. Since the ink does not dry right away, their writing hand sweeps over the words, and thus lefties run the risk of smearing the ink. The same applies to writing in clay or stone. Thus right-handed people, the vast majority in ancient times just as today, used their left hands in contact with the stone tablet. Because that was the hand with which they held the chisel, it made more sense to go from right to left. The same practice prevailed when they began writing with pens on parchment. That way, if the writer's hand slipped, the words already written were not spoiled. and the chance was greater that only the blank part would be affected.

2. Hebrew makes a comeback as a spoken language after almost twenty centuries

Hebrew was the language of the Israelites who sojourned in Egypt, were enslaved there, and were led forth by Moses.

Biblical Hebrew is the language of the Five Books of Moses, and the books of the Prophets and the Writings. Hebrew gradually ceased being a spoke language after 70 C.E., when the Jews were driven from the Land of Israel by the Romans and were scattered throughout the world. Of course, Hebrew remained alive, and was used constantly in other ways. It was the language of Jewish prayer, Jewish study, reading the Torah, and correspondence. Above all, it was used as the language of a tremendously rich literature of law, theology, philosophy, science, medicine, poetry, and grammar.

About 130 years ago a young man was inspired with a vision that Hebrew could once again live as a spoken language. His name was Eliezer Ben-Yehuda, and he went to work and write in the Land of Israel, then known as Palestine because this was decades before the founding of the State of Israel. At first he was thought an idle dreamer, but slowly and surely, something of the fire that burned within him spread to his friends and neighbors, then to wider and wider circles, until in a few years almost all the Jews in the land were speaking Hebrew! It went on to become the language of the State of Israel. One of the greatest miracles of modern times had come to pass. This was the first time in all human history that a language that had ceased being spoken in ancient times came back to life on the lips of men, women, and children.

One of the greatest problems Eliezer Ben-Yehuda faced was the lack of words in Hebrew for describing the complex culture of modern life. He single-handedly wrote a great dictionary of the Hebrew language, in seventeen volumes. Today, of course, Hebrew, along with Arabic, is an official language of the State of Israel. Israel has no one other than Eliezer Ben-Yehuda to thank for this.

3. Hebrew is the mother of practically all world alphabets used today

It might strike you as rather odd, but the actual historical fact is that the Hebrew-Phoenician alphabet is the mother of practically every alphabet now used in the world. The English alphabet is directly descended from the Hebrew-Phoenician alphabet and largely follows the order of the Hebrew alphabet. The names of the English letters are actually fragments of the old Hebrew words that were used as the names of the letters.

The Phoenicians lived just north of the Hebrews on a narrow strip of land hugging the ancient coast of Israel. The Hebrew language and the Phoenician language were practically identical. As the Phoenicians traveled westward, they met the Greeks, who to the amazement of the Phoenicians could not read or write. They proceeded to teach the Greeks the twenty-two letters of their alphabet. It was the old Hebrew alphabet that the Greeks borrowed and passed on to Latin, and it is the old Hebrew alphabet that the Greek alphabet most closely resembles. Greek used to be written as Hebrew is, from right to left. When the order was changed and they began to write from left to right, the Greeks turned many letters around. If you turn around some of the old Hebrew letters, you will see that they are almost identical to our present English letters. For example, an A lying on its side is the Old Hebrew aleph. Set it up straight and it is an A!

4. Hebrew words have three-letter roots, and Hebrew boasts the most famous word in any language

Practically every word in Hebrew goes back to a root, and this root almost always is made up of three consonants. You can do anything you want to the root. You can use it in any verb form or tense. You can turn it into any one of ten or twenty or more nouns. No matter what you do, you will always see, staring you in the face, the three consonants of the root. And no matter what you do with the root, the word will carry something of the meaning of the root. This is the beauty and the irresistible logic of word building in Hebrew, and by far the most fundamental law of the Hebrew language.

Here is an example of how the three-letter root system works, using the word amen.

The ancient Hebrews loved the word amen. They used it to express their every hope that God would be merciful to them and grant them their heart's desire. From Hebrew the word spread to over a thousand languages. It has entered more languages and is used in more countries than any other word in human speech.

The Hebrew root of amen is a-m-n. It means "confirm" or "support, and conveys the idea of being true and faithful, of being sure and certain in one's work. Here are some Hebrew words and their meanings derived from the root a-m-n:

> amen: may this prayer come true
> immun: training
> ne'eman: faithful
> emunah: fidelity
> amman: master workman
> ummanut: craftsmanship
> amnam, umnam: truly
> me'uman: trained
> omenet: foster mother

5. Biblical Hebrew names are still at the top of the list of names in use today

Biblical names continue to be used with great frequency in the naming of children, both Jewish and non-Jewish. What is even more interesting is that every biblical name has a distinct meaning, often unknown to the bearer of the name. Here is a brief list of some of the currently most popular biblical names in use in English nowadays. I have included the meaning of each name, some information about the biblical figure, and where the name can be found in the Bible for further exploration.

Aaron: meaning "messenger" or "mountain." He was the brother of Moses and Miriam, and founder of the Israelite priestly dynasty (Exodus 4).

Abigail: meaning "my father's joy." Variants include Abbie and Gail. Abigail was an early follower of David before he became king (I Samuel 25:14–42).

Abraham: meaning "father of a mighty nation." Abraham was Israel's first patriarch (Genesis 11:26–25:10).

Adam: meaning "man" or "red clay." He was the first human being created by God on the sixth day of creation (Genesis 1–3).

Amos: meaning "burdened" or troubled." Originally a shepherd boy, Amos became a prophet in the time of the Judean king Uzziah (Book of Amos).

Benjamin: meaning "son of my right hand." He was the youngest of Jacob's twelve sons by Rachel (Genesis 35:16–50:16).

Dan: meaning "he judged." He was the fifth son of Jacob by Bilhah, Rachel's handmaiden (Genesis 30:6–50:16).

Daniel: meaning "God is my judge." He was an Israelite prophet who as a youngster was taken to the court of the

Check Out Receipt

Saratoga Springs Public Library
518-584-7860
http://www.sspl.org

Tuesday, July 14, 2015 2:10:35 PM
15146

Title: The wind rises [DVD]
Material: New / Popular Video
Due: 07/21/2015

Title: Fitzcarraldo [DVD].
Material: Video
Due: 07/21/2015

Title: Birdman [DVD].
Material: New / Popular Video
Due: 07/21/2015

Thank You!

Babylonian king Nebuchadnezzar in order to be taught Chaldean culture (Book of Daniel).

David: meaning "beloved." He was Israel's second king (I Samuel 16–II Samuel).

Deborah: meaning "swarm of bees." She was both a judge and a prophet of Israel (Judges 4–5).

Dinah: meaning "judgment." The only recorded daughter of Jacob, by his wife Leah, she was raped by Shechem (Genesis 30:21, 24).

Elisheva: meaning "oath of God." Elizabeth is a variant. She was the wife of Aaron (Exodus 6:23).

Emanuel: meaning "God is with us." Manuel and Immanuel are variants. He was the child prophesied by Isaiah to be born to Ahaz (Isaiah 7:14–17).

Esther: meaning "a star." She was a Persian Jewish woman who saved the Jews from the evil decree of Haman (Book of Esther).

Hannah: meaning "grace." Variants include Ann, Anne, Anita, and Nancy. She was the mother of the prophet Samuel (I Samuel 1–2).

Isaac: meaning "laughter." He was the son of Abraham and the Israelites' second patriarch (Genesis 21–35:28).

Jacob: meaning "held by the heel" or "supplanter." He was the son of Isaac and Rebekah, twin brother of Esau, and third of the patriarchs (Genesis 25:23–49:33).

Joel: meaning "God is willing." He was a prophet who preached in Judea (Book of Joel).

Jonathan: Meaning "God has given." He was the first son of King Saul and a loyal friend to David (I Samuel 14–15).

Joseph: meaning "he will increase." He was the favored son of Jacob, known for his coat of many colors (Genesis 37:1–50:26).

Michael: meaning "who is like God?" He is one of the four archangels of God (Daniel 10:13–21).

Miriam: meaning "bitter sea." She was a prophet and the sister of Moses and Aaron (Numbers 12:10–15, 20:1).

Rachel: meaning "ewe." She was the daughter of Rebekah's brother Laban, the younger sister of Leah, and the favored wife of Jacob (Genesis 29–35).

Rebekah: meaning "to tie" or "to bind." She was the wife of Isaac and the mother of Jacob and Esau (Genesis 24–28).

Ruth: meaning "friendship." A Moabite woman, she was the daughter-in-law of Naomi and an ancestor of King David (Book of Ruth).

Samuel: meaning "God has heard." He was a prophet and the last of the Israelite judges (I and II Samuel).

Sarah: meaning "princess." She was the wife of Abraham and the Israelites' first matriarch (Genesis 11:29–23:1).

CHAPTER 2

Jewish Holidays

High Holy Days

1. Yom Kippur: Festival of chickens et al.

Yom Kippur is generally known as the Day of Atonement. In Leviticus 23:27 it is called Yom ha-Kippurim (literally, "Day of Atonements"), while in Leviticus 16:31 it is called Shabbat Shabbaton, "Sabbath of Solemn Rest." The Jerusalem Talmud (Rosh Hashanah 4:1) refers to Yom Kippur simply as Yoma, "The Day," which is also the name applied to the entire tractate dealing with the Day of Atonement.

In Babylon, Yom Kippur was called Yoma Rabbah, "The Great Day," and in Palestine centuries ago it was called Tzoma Rabbah, "The Great Fast." Today some refer to Yom Kippur as "The White Fast" in contradistinction to the Black Fast, another name for Tisha B'Av, which marks the destruction of the Jerusalem Temples.

Finally, Palestinian Arabs call Yom Kippur the "Festival of Chickens," for on the days preceding Yom Kippur they sell numerous white chickens to Orthodox Jews for the Kapparot atonement ceremony in which chickens are used to vicariously atone for transgressions.

2. The obligation to eat on Yom Kippur

Rabbi Shelomoh Goren, while serving as chief chaplain of the Israel Defense Forces, ordered that a soldier fighting in a battle on the Day of Atonement is obligated to eat if he feels his strength is declining in order not to jeopardize the outcome of the war. People in several other categories are also be given special dispensations on Yom Kippur.

> Sick people are required to follow doctor's orders. If a physician tells a patient to eat, the patient must do so even if he or she feels able to fast.

A pregnant woman is permitted to eat on Yom Kippur if she wishes to do so (Code of Jewish Law, Orach Chayim 617:2).

A new mother is in the same category as a seriously ill person for the first three days after childbirth and therefore is not allowed to fast (Orach Chayim 617:4).

Children nine years old or younger are not allowed to fast even if they want to because it might be harmful to their health.

The important consideration in all these cases is that the laws are made to live by, not to die by.

3. Jewish calendar ingenuity: Never on Sunday, Wednesday, or Friday

As a result of rabbinic calculations, the first day of Rosh Hashanah can never fall on a Sunday, Wednesday, or Friday. This was arranged so that Yom Kippur, the Day of Atonement, would neither immediately precede nor follow the Sabbath. The rationale was to eliminate the possibility of having two consecutive days on which it is forbidden by Jewish law to prepare food and to bury the dead. For a similar reason, Hoshana Rabbah, the holiday on which the worshipers beat willow branches, never occurs on the Sabbath. The rabbis arranged it this way so no one would ever be tempted to beat the willows on the holy Sabbath, when it would be a forbidden activity.

4. The shammash's wake-up call

During the month of Elul, in the days preceding Rosh Hashanah, it was the custom in some East European communities for the shammash (sexton) to personally go from house to

house and awaken the people to attend the Selichot peniten-
tial prayer service. Some sextons used special hammers to rap
on the doors of the villagers. Yemenite children have a custom of tying string to their feet and hanging one end out the
window. When the shammash made his rounds at midnight,
he pulled the string to waken the children, who would then
accompany him with small ram's horns and join in waking
the sleeping people.

5. The day the shofar stopped sounding

The sounding of the ram's horn is a legal requirement on
the High Holy Days. It is the Jewish wake-up call, reminding
people to do acts of repentance and change their ways. Rabbi
Shelomoh Goren, while serving as chief chaplain of the Israel
Defense Forces, ruled that soldiers near an enemy position
were religiously exempted from listening to the sounds of the
shofar because the shofar sounds would reveal their location.

6. An Islamic parallel to Yom Kippur

Yom Kippur was the model for the Muslim holiday known
as Ashura (literally "tenth"), a day of fasting instituted by
Muhammad to coincide with the tenth day of Tishri. In the
belief that the Jews fasted on the Day of Atonement to com-
memorate their victory over Pharaoh, Muhammad instituted
this holy day to mark his own victory when he entered the
holy city of Medina.

According to Jewish tradition, the second tablets of the
Law were given to Moses on Yom Kippur. Muslims believe
that the Koran was sent from heaven on the day of the Ashura fast.

7. Sins of the mouth

Of the forty-four sins enumerated in the Al Chet confessional prayer recited on Yom Kippur, twenty-two deal with sins related to the mouth. Among these are wronging our neighbor, confessing insincerely, mocking parents and teachers, using foul language, indulging in foolish talk, gossiping, eating and drinking improperly, and not keeping promises. From this array of sins one can easily see the power of words, and how they can be hurtful and lead a person to transgress.

8. Rosh Hashanah Omens

There are numerous omens related to the festival of Rosh Hashanah. Following are four of the more interesting ones for your reading pleasure:

> It is customary to eat certain symbolic foods on Rosh Hashanah, based on a talmudic dictum (Horayot 12a): "Abaye taught: Now that you have said that an omen is significant, each person should become accustomed to eating at the beginning of the year [i.e., on Rosh Hashanah] gourds, fenugreek, leeks, beets, and dates." In his commentary on the Talmud, Rashi (Keritut 6a) explains the symbolism of these things in two ways:. "Some of them grow and ripen early [and thus represent merits], while others are sweet-tasting and signify a sweet year."
>
> "Rabbi Z'vid taught: The first day of Rosh Hashanah, if it is hot, the entire year will be hot. If it is cold, the entire year will be cold" (Talmud, Baba Batra 147a).
>
> It is customary not to sleep in the daytime on Rosh Hashanah. The custom is based on a dictum in the Jerusalem Talmud: "If one sleeps at the beginning of the year, his guardian angel will sleep" (Darchei Moshe).

"Rabbi Ammi said: To ascertain whether you will live through the year or not, you should, during the ten days between Rosh Hashanah and Yom Kippur, kindle a lamp in a house where there is no draft. If the light continues to burn, you may be certain that you will live through the year" (Talmud, Horayot 12a)

Sukkot

1. Yuchi Indians observe Sukkot

The Yuchi Indian tribe of Oklahoma celebrates an eight-day festival each year that bears an amazing resemblance to the Jewish festival of Sukkot. The Yuchis begin their festival on the day of the full moon during the holy harvest month. Like the Jews, they, too, dwell in booths, which are covered by branches and foliage. In the Yuchi processional around the fire in the holy cultic area, they carry a large foliage-crested branch. During the celebration, these branches are shaken, much like the shaking of the four species.

2. The etrog: An original Garden of Eden fruit

According to one tradition, the etrog, not the apple, is the fruit that was eaten by Adam and Eve in the Garden of Eden. It was customary for women to bite off the pitom (tip) of the etrog after services on Hoshana Rabbah. Since this was the time when the etrog ritual of the Sukkot period ceased, the women were symbolically demonstrating that, unlike Eve, they had resisted the temptation to eat the etrog until it was no longer needed. The pitom on the etrog was placed under the pillow or near a woman who was experiencing a difficult labor in order to ease her excruciating pain.

3. Seventy oxen and Sukkot

In Temple times, centuries ago, in addition to the regular daily sacrifices, the wine and water libations, additional sacrifices were offered on each day of Sukkot. As prescribed in chapter 29 of the Book of Numbers, a different number of oxen was offered each day: thirteen on the first, twelve on the second, with the total decreasing by one on each successive day. The total number of oxen offered throughout the festival came to seventy, corresponding to the seventy nations that were descended from Noah and thus were the ancestors of all the nations of the world.

Hanukkah

1. The Halley's comet connection

In Hebrew, Hanukkah is sometimes called Chag Ha-Urim, the Festival of Lights, which makes sense, because the lighting of the menorah, also known as a hanukkiah, is the primary mitzvah. However, according to an astronomical theory, Halley's comet came very close to the earth's atmosphere in 165 B.C.E., the very time when the Maccabean revolt and the other Hanukkah events were actually taking place. The comet's tail was a wondrous light in the sky. According to the theory, it was seen by the Jews after the Maccabee victory over the Syrian Greeks. Because of this great light in the sky at the moment of victory, Hanukkah was ever after associated with light. And speaking of light, the Talmud (Shabbat 23b) teaches that one who scrupulously observes the kindling of the Hanukkah light will have children who are Torah scholars. And the Code of Jewish Law (Orach Chayim 67) states that because of their important role in the Hanukkah victory, women should follow the custom of not doing work while the lights of the hanukkiah are burning. (Some women have been known to put their candles in the freezer before lighting them, to make them burn longer!)

2. Thousand in a cave

During the war against the Syrian-Greeks, many people hid in the numerous caves that abound in the mountains of Judea. It once happened that the king's officers found out that a large group of Jews, numbering around one thousand, were hiding in a certain huge cave. They sent soldiers up there to attack them. It was the Sabbath day. The officers ordered the people to come out. The people defiantly responded: "No, we will not come out. We will not take up arms and break the Sabbath. We would rather die instead." The Syrians then attacked and killed every one of the thousand Jews, none of whom picked up a weapon to resist.

After this tragedy, Mattathias, the father of Judah Maccabee, instructed his people that from then on they were permitted to defend themselves if attacked on the Sabbath day,. But it was too late to save the thousand in the cave.

3. A year without Hanukkah?

Strangely enough, there will be no festival of Hanukkah in the year 3031 of the civil calendar. And in the year 3032, there will be two Hanukkah celebrations, one beginning in early January and the second later that same year in December. As if this were not enough of a quirk in reconciling the Hebrew and civil calendars, you should know that the first day of Hanukkah can never occur on a Tuesday.

4. A second Sukkot

According to the Book of Maccabees, the eight-day festival of Sukkot could not be properly observed in the Temple while the war against the Syrian-Greeks was in progress. When the Temple was liberated, Hanukkah was instituted to serve as a kind of second Sukkot, making up for the holiday that had been missed. During the rededication of the Temple, the Jews marched around with palm branches (lulavim) in their hands, just as we do today on Sukkot, singing praises to God. Here is the text from the Second Book of Maccabees (10:1–8) for you to see for yourself:

> The sanctuary was purified on the twenty-fifth of Kislev. This joyous celebration went on for eight days, it was like Sukkot, for they recalled how only a short time before they had kept the festival while living like animals in the mountains. So they carried lulavim and etrogim and they chanted hymns to God, who had triumphantly led them to the purification of the Temple. A measure was passed by the public assembly that the entire Jewish people should observe these days every year.

5. The coin connection

The First Book of Maccabees (15:6) records that when Judea gained its independence, King Antiochus declared to Simon Maccabee: "I turn over to you the right to make your own stamp for coinage for your country." Before this the Judeans did not have the freedom to mint their own coins, and thus the first Jewish coins in history were issued as a result of Jewish independence.

Speaking of coins, in 1958 the Bank of Israel initiated a program of striking commemorative coins for use as Hanukkah gelt. The first Hanukkah coin portrayed exactly the same menorah that had appeared on the last of the Maccabean coins of Antigonus some two thousand years earlier. In 1976, the year of America's bicentennial and two-hundredth year of independence, the Israeli Hanukkah coin featured a colonial American menorah!

6. Hanukkah and playing cards

The practice of playing cards on Hanukkah began about six hundred years ago. It was customary for yeshiva students to abandon their studies to celebrate the holiday. One way the students expressed the joyous spirit of the day was to play games of chance. Rabbi Levi Yitzchak of Berdichev defended the practice by explaining that playing cards on Hanukkah nights would train them to stay up late, which would enable them to study Torah for longer hours throughout the year.

Purim

1. The Queen Esther–Hadassah connection

Esther's Hebrew name in the Book of Esther is Hadassah, the same as that of the famous Zionist organization for women. People often ask whether there is a connection between the name of the Hadassah organization and Queen Esther.

There is. After a visit to Palestine, the great Jewish leader Henrietta Szold decided to start a Zionist organization for women. She envisioned this group working for the health of women and children in what was later to become the State of Israel. The founding meeting was held at Temple Emanu-EL in New York. The date was Purim and the year was 1912. The women constituted themselves as the Hadassah chapter

of the Daughters of Zion. Eventually, the name would simply
become Hadassah.

2. No God in the Scroll of Esther

Believe it or not, God is not mentioned even one single time
in the Book of Esther. There are many explanations of why
this is so. According to one, Esther pleaded with the spiritual
leaders of her day to record the historical event in which she
had been involved, so that future generations would value
her supreme dedication to God and her people. The rabbis
therefore related the story as an historical event in which Esther was the heroine, and they were not explicit about the
part God played in the miracle. Thus the name of God does
not appear in the narrative.

Another explanation points out that Esther married King
Ahasuerus, a non-Jew, in the Purim story. This intermarriage
was God's unique way of saving the Jewish people from annihilation in this particular situation, but what if people had
concluded that intermarriage was always acceptable? The in-
clusion of God's name in the Book of Esther might have im-
plied that God sanctions intermarriage. Thus, God was not
mentioned in the Scroll of Esther.

Some rabbinic commentators discovered allusions to God
concealed in the Book of Esther. For instance, the name of
God (YHVH) is formed by the initial letters of four successive
words when read backward: Hi ve-chol ha-nashim yitnu ("it,
and all the women will give") In the Book of Esther, the name
of God (YHVH) is formed by the final letters of four successive words when read backward: zeh eynennu shoveh li ("this
gives satisfaction to me").

Finally, the word yehudim (Hebrew for "Jews") occurs

thirty-eight times in the Book of Esther. Thirty-two times it is spelled in the traditional way: yod, hay, vav, dalet, yud, mem. The other six times, however, an extra yud is inserted before the final letter mem, so that there are two yods together (Esther 4:7, 8:1, 8:7, 8:13, 9:15, 9:18). Some commentators assert that the extra yod in six places is intentional, alluding to God's Presence. The letter yud by itself means yad ("hand"). And two yuds in succession is a common abbreviation for God's name. Together, the reasoning goes, the combined meaning of the double yud is "the hand of God."

3. The longest verse in the Bible

The longest verse in the Bible is found in the Book of Esther: chapter 8, verse 9. The original text in Hebrew contains a total of forty-three words! Here is the verse in translation:

> So the king's scribes were summoned at that time, on the twenty-third of the third month, that is, in the month of Sivan; and letters were written, at Mordecai's dictation, to the Jews and to the satraps, the governors and the officials of the one hundred and twenty-seven provinces from India to Ethiopia: to every province in its own script and to every people in its own language, and to the Jews in their own script and language.

4. Special Purims

Over the centuries a custom arose that whenever a Jewish community was saved from its enemies, it would celebrate the event annually with a special local Purim. A celebration of this kind was known as Purim Katan, "Little Purim." The celebration, held on the anniversary of the day the community was saved, was modeled after that of Purim. It included fasting the day before, reading a megillah (scroll) that recounted the story of the community's salvation, reciting the Al ha-Nissim prayer, and holding a special feast. The Encyclopaedia Judaica lists more than a hundred special Purims. Here are ten of them:

Purim of Algiers (Purim Edom): Established in 1540, and observed on the fourth of Cheshvan, in commemoration of being saved from destruction in the Spanish Algerian wars of 1516–17 and 1542.

Baghdad Purim: Established in 1822 and observed on the eleventh of Av, it commemorates being relieved from Persian oppression in 1733.

Belgrade Purim: Established in 1822 and observed on the nineteenth of Sivan, it commemorates being saved from destruction during the Turko-Serbian war.

Cairo Purim (Purim Mitzrayim): Established in 1524 and observed on the twenty-eighth of Adar, it commemorates being saved from extermination.

Castille Purim (Purim Martinez): Established in 1339 and observed on the first of Adar, it commemorates being saved from annihilation following accusations by the Jew-baiter Gonzales Martinez, the king's adviser.

Prague Purim: Established in 1620 and observed on the fourteenth of Cheshvan, it commemorates being saved from a pogrom by Emperor Ferdinand II

Roman Purim: Established in 1793 and observed on the first of Shevat, it commemorates the ghetto being saved from assault and fire.

Sarajevo Purim: Established in 1819 and commemorated on the fourth of Cheshvan, it commemorates the release of ten leaders of the Jewish community from prison and execution.

Vilna Purim: Established in 1794 and observed on the fifteenth of Av, it commemorates being saved from destruction during the Russo-Polish war.

Galicia Purim: The exact date of its establishment is not known. Observed on the twelfth of Tevet, it commemorates being saved from annihilation because of a blood libel accusation.

5. It's "kosher," and it's in the Book of Esther

Believe it or not, the only time the Hebrew word kasher ("kosher") appears in the entire Bible is in Esther 8:5: " 'If it please Your Majesty,' she said, 'and if I have won your favor and the proposal seems right (kasher) to Your Majesty . . .' "

In this context kasher means "correct" or "proper," and has nothing to do with food, in which the same word plays a large role in Jewish law.

There are some other interesting occurrences in the Book of Esther that make it unique. For instance, all of the letters of the Hebrew alphabet can be found in chapter 3, verse 13. And the word mishteh, meaning "party" or "banquet," occurs twenty different times.

6. The test of sobriety

According to the Jewish thinker Abudraham in medieval Spain, one is required on Purim to drink enough wine so that one becomes too intoxicated to be able to compare two columns of figures to determine whether or not they are equal. The Talmud expresses the same idea tersely as the difference between Arur Haman ("cursed is Haman") and Baruch Mordecai ("blessed is Mordecai"). Both of these phrases in Jewish numerology have the same numerical value—502!

7. Humongous Hamantasche

The Guinness Book of World Records has made it official. Seventeen students at the Hadassah Hotel Management College in Jerusalem have baked the world's largest hamantasche. The triangular cookie weighed 550 pounds and included 198 pounds of flour, 350 eggs, 17.6 pounds of poppy seed, and 50.6 pounds of margarine. It was 4.5 feet long and 3.5 feet high. The hamantache was split in two. Half went to the children of Hadassah's Children's Pavilion on Mount Scopus, and the rest was given to Ethiopian students at a Hadassah preparatory course in Jerusalem.

Passover

1. Where is Moses in the Passover Haggadah?

Believe it or not, Moses, Judaism's most important prophet and the key player in the story of the Exodus from Egypt, is only mentioned explicitly one single time in all of the Haggadah. His absence reflects the intention of the rabbis to give sole credit to God for the deliverance of the Israelites from Egypt. Omitting Moses from the Haggadah was a way of preventing possible hero-worship of him.

2. A Calendar Oddity

The Jewish calendar is arranged such that the first day of Passover will never ever fall on a Monday, Wednesday, or Friday. Furthermore, the first six days of Passover always determine the days of the week when the other festivals will occur. This has been fixed by the device of combining the first six letters of the Hebrew alphabet with the last six letters in reverse order. This results in the following combinations:

> The first day of Passover will fall on the same first day of the Fast of the Ninth of Av
>
> The second day of Passover will fall on the same day as the second day of Shavuot
>
> The third day of Passover will fall on the same day as Rosh Hashanah
>
> The fourth day of Passover will fall on the same day as Simchat Torah
>
> The fifth day of Passover will fall on the same day as Yom Kippur
>
> The sixth day of Passover will fall on the same day as the previous Purim
>
> The seventh day of Passover will fall on the same day as Israel Independence Day

3. Interesting Yachatz customs

Yachatz, the breaking of the middle matzah, is the fourth part of every Passover Seder. The usual American custom is to break the middle matzah and hide a piece of it for the afikoman. But there are many other interesting matzah customs related to this part of the Seder. For instance, Jewish mystics, the kabbalists, broke the middle matzah on the Seder table into the shape of the Hebrew letters dalet and vav, the fourth and sixth letters of the Hebrew alphabet. According to Jewish numerology (gematria), this makes a total of ten, equaling the number of sefirot—the emanations of God's light or mystical spheres in the universe.

Among Moroccan families, the middle matzah is broken into two pieces to resemble the Hebrew letter hey, which stands for God. While the matzah is broken, everyone sings an Arabic song that recalls the miracle of the Red Sea. The hey-shaped matzah is then taken by each member of the family and held against their eyes while Ha lachma anya ("This is the bread of affliction") is recited.

4. Prayer for eating chametz on Passover

The eating of chametz (leavened foods) is strictly forbidden during Passover. Traditional Jews go to extraordinary lengths to rid their homes of any leavened products. This makes all the more remarkable something that happened during World War II. It is not surprising that on Passover of 1944 there was no matzah to be had in the Bergen-Belsen concentration camp. Nor is it surprising that the rabbis among the Jewish prisoners said that it was permitted to eat leavened food, for they knew full well that prisoners were severely undernourished, and if they did not eat would surely die of starvation. What may be surprising, however, is that the rabbis told the prisoners to recite a special prayer before eating chametz. Here is the prayer as it now appears in some modern Haggadahs.

> Our Father, it is known to You that it is our wish to do Your will and to celebrate Passover by eating matzah and not eating chametz. But our heart is pained because our enslavement prevents us and we are in danger of our lives. Behold, we are ready to fulfill Your mitzvah: "And you shall live by My laws, and not die by them." We pray to You that You may keep us alive and redeem us soon so that we may observe Your laws with a perfect heart. Amen.

5. The Hillel matzah sandwich

In the twentieth century the revivers of the Hebrew language began to study possible terms for the word "sandwich." They first suggested calling it a hillelit, named after Hillel, the head of the ancient Sanhedrin, just as the English "sandwich" was named after the Earl of Sandwich. Later, they settled on the word karich, from korech, the verb that designates the original sandwich eaten by Hillel in the Passover Seder.

Shavuot

1. Honey and the Hebrew alphabet

A medieval Jewish custom connected Jewish education with Shavuot. On Shavuot, young children who were starting school would be brought to the classroom for the very first time. They were shown a slate with the letters of the Hebrew alphabet covered with honey or candy. As the child learned the Hebrew letters, he was allowed to lick off the honey or eat the candy, thus fulfilling the biblical verse "How pleasing is Your word to my palate, sweeter than honey" (Psalm 119:103) There are still quite a number of religious schools that continue this custom, or a variation on it, to this day.

2. Cheese Sunday

A Shavuot custom that has a counterpart in gentile usage is the eating of dairy dishes, especially cheese. The usual explanation of this custom is quite fanciful. In Psalm 68:15, the mountain on which the Torah is given is described as "a mountain divine, a Bashan-like mountain, a mount of gavnunnim, a Bashan-like mount." The word gavnunnim means "gibbous" or "multipeaked," but it was fancifully connected with the Hebrew gevinah, "cheese," the conception of a mountain made of cheese being commonplace in folk tales.

Accordingly, it was maintained that the eating of cheese was a reminder of the giving of the Torah at this season. Similarly, dairy dishes are commonly consumed on the analogous Scottish harvest festival of Beltane on May 1, and churning and cheese making are a common features of the celebration. In Macedonia, the Sunday before Lent is known as Cheese Sunday!

3. Arab Shavuot

Jewish communities in Arab countries observe the Shavuot custom of having someone ascend to the roof of the synagogue and throw apples down to the people in the street below. The origin of this custom is traced to the notion that there is a similarity between the exclamation of the children of Israel at Mount Sinai and the growth of an apple. The fruit of the apple begins to develop before the leaf. Similarly, as stated in Exodus 24:7, the children of Israel proclaimed na'ase ve-nishma, "we will do and we will listen," whereas the more logical order would have been, "We will first listen and then we will act." They were announcing their resolution to perform the mitzvot before they analyzed them.

4. Confirmation: A Reform innovation

Reform Jews introduced the custom of the confirmation ceremony for sixteen-year-olds at Shavuot. The Reform rabbinate had concluded that in the conditions of modern society, where children do not become independent adults or even take on a more independent emotional and intellectual life at age thirteen, it was important to add to the Bar/Bat Mitzvah some way to recognize a later state of development. In the early German Reform synagogues, confirmation of boys began in 1810 and of girls in 1817. At first there was no set day, but gradually the practice focused on Shavuot. On Shavuot in 1846, at a German Reform synagogue on Henry Street in New York City, the youngsters sang psalms, heard the rabbi exhort them to adhere to Judaism, and received a blessing from their parents and their rabbi. Today, many Conservative, Reform, and Reconstructionist synagogues have Shavuot confirmation ceremonies for their teenage graduates of Hebrew high school.

5. Shavuot Wedding

Shavuot has often been portrayed metaphorically as the marriage between God and the children of Israel. The most concrete expression of this imagery is the Sephardic custom of writing a marriage contract (ketubah) between God and the Jewish people. The language is adapted from the traditional ketubah and is read after the ark is opened and before the Torah scrolls are removed from it during the Torah service. The ketubah is often read under the traditional wedding canopy (chuppah). Here are selections from the Sephardic ketubah for Shavuot:

> Friday, the sixth of Sivan, the day appointed by God for the revelation of the Torah to His beloved people. . . . The Invisible One came forth from Sinai, shone from Seir, and appeared from Mount Paran unto all the kinds of the earth. In the year 2448 since the creation of the world, the era by which we are accustomed to reckon in this land whose foundations were upheld by God, as it is written: "For God has founded it upon the seas and established it upon the floods" (Psalm 24:2) The Bridegroom (God), Ruler of rulers, Prince of princes, Distinguished among the select, whose mouth is pleasing to all of

whom is delightful, said to the pious, lovely, and virtuous maiden (the people of Israel) who won His favor above all women, who is beautiful as the moon, radiant as the sun, awesome as bannered hosts: Many days you will you be Mine and I will be your Redeemer. Behold, I have sent you gold precepts through the lawgiver Jekuthiel (Moses). Be thou My mate according to the law of Moses and Israel, and I will honor, support, and maintain you and be your shelter and refuge in everlasting mercy. And I will set aside for you, in lieu of your virginal faithfulness, the life-giving Torah by which you and your children will live in health and tranquility. The bride (Israel) consented and became God's spouse.

Thus an eternal covenant, binding them forever, was established between them. The bridegroom then agreed to add to the above all future expositions of Scripture, including Sifra, Sifre, Aggadah and Tosefta. He established the primacy of the 248 commandments which are incumbent upon all, and added to them the 365 negative commandments. The dowry that the bride brought from the house of her father consists of an understandingheart that understands, ears that hearken, and eyes that see. Thus the sum total of the contract and the dowry, with the addition of the positive and negative commandments, amounts to the following: "Revere God and observe God's commandments: this applied to all mankind" (Ecclesiastes 12:13). The bridegroom desiring to confer privileges upon God's people Israel and to transmit these valuable assets to them, took upon Himself the responsibility of this marriage contract, to be paid from the best portions of His property. All these conditions are valid and established forever and forever. The bridegroom has given His oath to carry them out in favor of His people and to enable those that love God to inherit substance. Thus God has given His oath. The bridegroom has followed the legal formality of symbolic delivery of this document, which is bigger than the earth and broader than the seas. Everything then, is firm, clear and established. I invoke heaven and earth as reliable witnesses.

May the bridegroom rejoice with the bride whom God has taken as His lot and may the bride rejoice with the Husband of her youth while uttering words of praise.

6. Tikkun leyl Shavuot

A legendary source has it that on the night preceding the giving of the Torah, many of the children of Israel went complacently to sleep when one would think they were too excited to sleep because of eager anticipation for the unfolding of the most world-shaking event in human history. This indifference was an affront to God. In order to amend the wrong of our ancestors, Jews remain awake the entire night before Shavuot, awaiting the dawn of the next day, when they will celebrate the receiving of the Torah at Mount Sinai. Today, in many traditional settings, people study Torah texts the whole night through.

7. Judgment of trees

According to the Mishnah (Rosh Hashanah 1:2), it is on Shavuot that the trees and their fruits are judged by God, who decides whether the year will be one of abundance or scarcity. In ancient times this judgment affected the quality of the first fruits (bikkurim) brought to the Temple. The synagogue is typically decorated on Shavuot with plants and bushes to remind us to pray that trees yield an abundance of fruit, which would add honor to the donor of the first fruits.

8. Shavuoslech—Little Shavuots

In Eastern Europe, a special art form emerged in connection with Shavuot that has since become widespread: paper cutouts, called shavuoslech (literally "little Shavuots") or raize-lech ("little roses"). The custom may have developed when some rabbis tried to stop the custom of bringing greenery into the synagogue, fearing it was too like a pagan habit. Seeking an acceptable form of decoration, Lithuanian Jews chose the paper cutout as a way of showing greenery and flowers, letting the light shine through the cutouts in their windows.

9. Shavuot customs around the world

On some nonreligious kibbutzim in Israel, the custom on Shavuot is to bring all the newborn children to a festive gathering and display them for everyone to see, along with all of the new first fruits of the spring harvest season. Some synagogues today are also known to extend a special invitation to parents with newborns on Shavuot.

On Shavuot the Samaritans visit their holy places on Mount Gerizim: Givat Ola, where Moses's tabernacle stood; Isaac's altar, where Abraham bound his son Isaac; and the site of the twelve rocks that Joshua placed before erecting Moses' tabernacle.

The Kurdistan Jews call Shavuot Ziyara ("Making a Pilgrimage"). On this day they visit the tombs of many famous people, including the tomb of the prophet Nachum.

On the evening of the eighth day of Passover, Algerian Jews buy green corn from the Arabs and suspend it from the ceilings in their homes. They let it hang there until Shavuot, and during the counting of the omer, they all eat of the corn together with a sort of pancake, first dipping both of these in milk.

In the holy city of Jerusalem, thousands of Jews who have studied Torah the whole night of Shavuot walk down to the

Western Wall at the break of dawn to recite the morning service.

It was the custom in Mainz, Germany, on Shavuot to bake specially sweetened challot called "Sinai loaves." They were given this name because on Shavuot the children of Israel began the study of Torah, and the receiving of the Torah was made sweet for them.

In Frankfurt-am-Main, Germany, it was customary on Shavuot to partake of a specially prepared dairy or meat dish fashioned like a ladder with seven steps, in memory of the seven heavens that God opened for Israel at the time of the giving of the Torah.

The Ashkenazic custom of eating dairy foods on Shavuot derived from the belief that the Israelites knew nothing of the dietary laws before the Torah was given. Once they received the Torah they realized that their utensils and meat supply were unkosher, and so instead ate dairy. Yemenite Jews never adopted the custom of eating dairy foods on Shavuot because they followed the midrashic statement that Abraham, the first Jew, observed all 613 commandments and handed down this tradition to his progeny.

Finally, in Romania, Shavuot is commonly known as Rusaliile. This word designated three ancient princesses who were forced to remain unmarried. In revenge, they return to earth for three days each year to plague humanity, destroy the harvest, and blow away the roofs of houses. During this period no manual work may be performed, no one may smile, and children may not make faces. To exorcise the malicious ladies, branches of wormwood are placed under the pillow at night or worn in the belt.

CHAPTER **3**

Unusual Superstitions

Every Jewish community throughout the centuries has generated its own peculiar folklore and associated practices. Folklore often includes a variety of superstitions. For contemporary Jews, superstition and folklore are foundations of warm sentimental waters, evoking memories of parents and grandparents who often warned us of things not to do and things to avoid. As strange and sometimes silly as many of these warnings sounded, they were intended to safeguard us from danger and the evil that was believed to lurk everywhere. In this chapter you will learn about some superstitions and Jewish folkloric belief that undoubtedly you never knew existed.

1. Folkloristic superstitions and circumcision

Because of the relatively high rate of infant mortality and sickness centuries ago, many protective customs arose that were intended to protect mother and son at the circumcision. Here are some of the more interesting ones:

Place red ribbons and garlic on a baby's crib to ward off evil spirits.

Place a knife under the mother's pillow the night before the bris to protect her from evil spirits.

During a difficult labor, place a Torah belt around the mother's belly to protect her.

Put candy under the mother's bed to draw the attention of evil spirits away from her and the baby.

During the Middle Ages, it was customary to "cradle" the baby boy after his circumcision. In this ceremony, a copy of the Five Books of Moses was placed upon the baby in his cradle. The people gathered around him and would say: "May this child fulfill what is written in this book!"

Throw sugar, raisins, cake, and coins into the baby's cradle before the child is placed in it, as an omen for a sweet and abundant life.

2. Naming-a-child superstitions and customs

Following are some of the customs and superstitious actions connected to the naming of a child:

Postpone the naming of a child (because it was feared that the name was a "handle" with which the Angel of Death could grasp the baby).

Never marry a person who has the same name as your mother or father (out of fear that the Angel of Death might confuse two persons with the same name, leading to the premature death of one or the other).

Give a child an extra name that symbolizes length of years, such as the Yiddish name Alter, meaning "old person." Giving a name of this kind was believed to increase the child's longevity.

Change the name of a person who is very ill and near death to something that will deceive the Angel of Death. The usual name in such cases was Chayim or Chaya (the masculine and feminine forms of the word "life") .

3. Wedding customs and superstitions

Over the centuries a belief emerged that weddings were especially susceptible times for evil spirits to be lurking. Accordingly, a series of protective customs emerged. Here are some of them:

Have the bride circle around the groom seven times. The circling action is a protection against evil spirits and demons.

Carry a lighted torch or candle to fool the evil forces. (This is still seen today in many traditional Jewish wedding ceremonies.)

Break a glass at the end of the wedding ceremony as a protective measure against the forces of evil spirits and demons.

Have the bride and groom fast on the day of their wedding. This will fool the evil spirits into thinking that it is a day of mourning rather than one of ultimate joy.

Break a dish when announcing the engagement to frighten away the evil spirits.

Get married on a Tuesday. This is an auspicious day for a wedding because in the biblical creation story God twice says on the third day (i.e., Tuesday) "it was good."

4. Superstitions and death

Here are some still widely followed customs related to death and dying in the Jewish tradition. All are meant to protect from evil spirits and demons.

Make seven stops before lowering the casket into the ground at the cemetery.

Pour out household water from the house of the mourner. Evil spirits cannot cross the water, and thus the soul of the departed will not be trapped inside the house.

Before burial, watch over and care for a deceased corpse, and read psalms in its presence.

On leaving a cemetery, pluck some blades of grass and throw them behind you to repel the evil spirits that lurk in such places.

5. Jewish superstitious numerology

The power of numbers was a favorite subject of speculation in the ancient world. The occult potency of numbers was recognized and was given an honored place in Jewish superstition. The common superstition that there is good fortune in odd numbers found its Jewish version in the talmudic belief that even numbers are unlucky and dangerous. Following are examples of the use of numbers in Jewish superstition.

Number Two

Do not do two things at one time or repeat any action, such as taking fire twice from a hearth, when there is an invalid in the house.

An unhappy fate will befall two couples who know each other and are married on the same day.

To marry off two children at one time or two sisters or brothers in one week, or indeed, to celebrate any two weddings within a week, is to invite trouble.

Do not visit the same grave twice in one day.

Number Three

Actions and incantations were to be performed three hours before sunrise, three days before the new moon, or three days in succession.

Diviners could obtain answers to only three questions at one time.

To avert the evil eye, spit three times on your fingertips and each time make a quick movement in the air with your hand.

Because evil spirits prey on the souls of little boys and disregard little girls, a boy's hair is allowed to grow until he is three years old so that he will be indistinguishable from a girl.

Number Seven

The bride or groom circles the other under the wedding canopy seven times because a closed circle can repel evil demons.

To cure a fever, take seven prickles from seven palm trees, seven chips from seven beams, seven nails from seven bridges, seven ashes from seven ovens, seven scoops of earth from seven door sockets, seven pieces of pitch from seven ships, seven handfuls of cumin, and seven hairs from the beard of an old dog, and tie them to the neck.

After a funeral, the homeward procession should stop seven times in order to confuse and shake off any evil spirits that follow.

6. A potpourri of Jewish superstitions

Here are a number of other Jewish superstitious practices that are still in vogue in modern times.

Demons like the sound of whistling. Do not whistle in your house; this will make it less attractive to demons. (This custom is traceable to the Kiev area of Ukraine in the early nineteenth century.)

Chew on thread if you are wearing a garment on which someone is actively sewing. This folkloristic custom is related to the practice of sewing the remains of a deceased person into a burial shroud. By chewing on a garment while someone is sewing, you show that you are very much alive and in this world.

Expectorating is an ancient way of repelling evil spirits. Today, saying the phrase "pooh, pooh, pooh" (as if one were spitting) after witnessing something wonderful or beautiful, such as a newborn baby, is considered an antidote to evil.

You are protected from harm while involved in performing a mitzvah. Giving charity to the poor is a mitzvah. Therefore, when someone leaves on a long trip, especially to Israel, give that person some money to be given as charity on reaching the destination. The traveler will be protected while on the way to do the mitzvah.

It is bad luck to count Jews. In the Bible, counting for a census was often followed by a plague. In addition, counting people attracts the attention of the Angel of Death. In many traditional synagogues they do not count to see whether there are enough people to constitute a minyan, the prayer quorum of ten adults. Instead they recite a ten-word liturgical sentence. There is one word for each person; if you don't have a minyan, you can't finish the sentence. One such Hebrew phrase is Hoshi'a et ammecha u-varech et nachalatecha, u-rem ve-nasse'em ad ha-olam ("Bless and deliver Your people, Your heritage, sustain them forever").

Closing prayerbooks that were left open is a superstitious practice still seen in many synagogues. It probably derives from the ancient belief that an open book can be taken over by an evil spirit who will distort its meaning.

Do not walk on a threshold if you want to avoid the evil demons who reside within it.

Salt is an antidote to evil spirits. Put salt in your home or your pocket to eradicate them.

Metal has protective powers. Some Jewish people today like to wear or carry a metal pin because it has the power to repel evil spirits.

Three things take away a person's eyesight: combing one's hair while it is dry, drinking the drippings of wine, and putting on shoes while your feet are wet (Talmud, Pesachim 111b).

When you are frightened even though you don't see anything frightening, it is because your planet sees it. The remedy is to recite the Shema prayer (Talmud, Megillah 3a).

If you get sick, don't speak of it the first day, lest your luck get worse. After the first day you can speak freely about your illness (Talmud, Berachot 55b).

CHAPTER 4

Dreams

Almost everyone dreams, and it has been established that dreams are a necessary outlet for the mind. From the earliest of times, dreams have tantalized people with their secrets. They were often thought to be signs or messages from divine powers. The ancient Babylonians had implicit trust in dreams as a means of guidance. On the eve of important decisions they slept in a temple, hoping for dream counsel.

Professional dream interpreters were prominent in ancient Mesopotamia and Egypt, and manuals have revealed hundreds of dream interpretations. The interpretation of dreams has been a major component since the inception of that discipline.

On the whole, the Bible says remarkably little on the subject of dream interpretation. Only Joseph and Daniel engage in it, and both give the credit unreservedly to God. There is much about dreams in the Talmud. Berachot 55b records that there were twenty-four professional interpreters of dreams in Jerusalem, clearly an indication that the masses believed in the power and symbolism of dreams.

Many famous talmudic rabbis discussed dreams and enunciated doctrines concerning them. Yochanan ben Zakkai, for example, once dreamed that his sister's sons would lose 700 denarii. He therefore pressed them to give alms frequently, so that they would lose that sum piecemeal in a noble way (Talmud, Baba Batra 10a).

Diametrically opposed views on dreams were also expressed by rabbinic sages. Jonathan stated that "a man is shown in a dream only what is suggested by his own thoughts" (Talmud, Berachot 55b). This statement corresponds to the view of Freud, who asserted that thoughts repressed during the day may reappear and find fulfillment in a dream. As the Talmud (Berachot 55b) asserts, "A dream is only the result of the thought pondered during the day," and quotes Rava as saying that this is proven by the fact that "a person never sees in a dream a tree of gold or an elephant passing through the eye of a needle." In other words, far-fetched thoughts are not likely to be envisioned in a dream.

In rabbinic times it was customary to fast when one had a bad dream. This fast was known as a ta'anit chalom. Rav once asserted: "Fasting is as potent against a dream as fire is against a tow [a type of fiber used as a wick]" (Talmud, Shabbat 11a).

Here is a list from Berachot 56b–57b of symbols found in dreams and what they represent. Perhaps you will find them useful in understanding your own dreams.

If you see a reed in a dream, you may hope for wisdom. If you see several reeds, hope for understanding. A pumpkin, a palm heart, and a reed are all auspicious in a dream. It has been taught that pumpkins are shown in a dream only to those who fear heaven with all their might.

There are five sayings in connection with an ox in a dream. If you dream that you eat of its flesh, you will become rich; if that an ox has gored you, you will have sons who will contend together in the study of Torah; if that an ox bit you, sufferings will come upon you; if that the ox kicked you, you will have to go on a long journey; if that you rode upon an ox, you will rise to greatness.

If you see a donkey in a dream, you may hope for salvation.

If you see grapes in a dream, and they are white, whether in season or not in season, they are a good sign; if black, in season, they are a good sign. If they are not in season, they are a bad sign.

If you see a white horse in a dream, whether walking gently or galloping, it is a good sign. If a red horse, if walking gently, it is a good sign. If galloping, it is a bad sign.

If you see Ishmael in a dream, your prayer will be heard. And it must be Ishmael the son of Abraham, but not an ordinary Arab. If you see a camel in your dream, your death has been decreed by heaven but you have been delivered from it.

If you see Pinchas in a dream, a miracle will be wrought for you. If you see an elephant in a dream, a miracle will be wrought for you. If several elephants, wonders of wonders will be wrought for you. The elephants are a good sign if saddled, but a bad omen if not saddled.

If you see the words of a funeral oration, mercy will be granted to you from heaven and you will be redeemed. This is only if you see the words in writing. If in a dream you respond "May his great name be blessed," be assured that you have a place in the world-to-come. If you dream that you are reciting the Shema, you are worthy of the Divine Presence resting upon you, but your generation is not deserving enough. If you dream that you are putting on phylacteries, you may look forward to greatness. If you dream that you are praying, it is a good sign, provided that you do not complete the prayer.

If you see wheat in a dream, you will see peace. If you see barley in a dream, your iniquities will depart.

If you see a vine laden with fruit in a dream, your wife will not have a miscarriage. If you see a choice vine, you may look forward to seeing the Messiah.

If you see a fig tree in a dream, your learning will be preserved within you.

If you see pomegranates in a dream, and they are small, your business will be fruitful like a pomegranate. If big, your business will increase like a pomegranate. If they are split open, and you are a scholar, you may hope to study more Torah. If you are not learned, you may hope to perform more mitzvot.

If you see olives in a dream, and they are small, your business will continue to prosper, increasing like an olive. This is if you see the fruits. If you see the tree, you will have many sons. Some say that if you see an olive in your dream you will acquire a good name. If you see palm trees in a dream, your transgressions will come to an end.

If you see a goat in a dream, your will have a blessed year. If several goats, several blessed years.

If you see myrtle in a dream, you will have good luck with your property. If you have no property, you will inherit some from elsewhere.

If you see an etrog in a dream, you are honored in the sight of your Maker. If you see a palm branch in a dream, you are single-hearted in devotion to your Father in heaven.

If you see a goose in a dream, then you may hope for wisdom. He who dreams of being with a goose will be head of an academy.

If you see a rooster in a dream, you may expect a male child. If several roosters, several sons. If you see a hen in a dream, a fine garden and rejoicing. If you see eggs in a dream, your petition remains in suspense. If they are broken, your petition will be granted. The same with nuts and cucumbers and all vessels of glass and all breakable things like these.

If you dream that you are entering a large town, your desire will be fulfilled.

If you dream that you are shaving your head, it is a good sign for you. If your head and your beard, it is a good sign for you and your whole family.

If you dream that you are sitting in a small boat, you will acquire a good name. If in a large boat, both you and your family will acquire one, but this is only if it is on the high seas.

If you dream that you are going up to a roof, you will attain a high position. If that you are going down, you will be degraded. Abaye and Rava, however, both say that once you have attained a high position you will remain there.

If you dream that you are tearing your garments, the evil

decree against you will be torn up. If you dream that you are standing naked, if this happens in Babylon, you will remain sinless, but if in the Land of Israel, you will be naked of pious needs. If you dream that you will be arrested by the police, protection will be offered you. If you dream that you have been put in neck chains, additional protection will be afforded you. This is only if you dream of neck chains, not of mere rope. If you dream that you walk into a marsh, you will become head of an academy.

If you see a serpent in a dream, it means that your livelihood is assured. If it bites you, it means that it will be doubled. If you kill it, you will lose your sustenance.

There are three kings who are significant in a dream. If you see David in a dream, hope for piety. If Solomon, hope for wisdom. If Achav, fear for punishment.

There are three prophets of significance for dreams. If you see the Book of Kings, look for greatness. If Ezekiel, look forward to wisdom. If Isaiah, look forward to consolation. If Jeremiah, fear punishment.

If you see the Book of Job in a dream, fear punishment. If you see the Scroll of Esther, a miracle will occur for you.

All animals are a good sign in a dream except the elephant, the monkey, and the long-tailed ape.

All metal implements are a good sign in a dream except a hoe, a mattock, and a hatchet.

All fruits are a good sign in a dream except unripe grapes. All vegetables are a good sign in a dream except turnip tops.

All colors except blue are a good sign in a dream.

All birds are a good sign in a dream except the owl, the horned owl, and the bat.

CHAPTER 5

Demons, Spirits, and Evil Forces

Protecting themselves against evil spirits and demons was a great concern of all people in the ancient Near East. Demons (mazzikim in Hebrew), as messengers of the lord of the underworld, were believed to live in the wilderness and near graves. Many of them were spirits of the dead, especially of persons who had died a violent death or had not been properly buried. Sometimes even sickness was thought to be caused by demonic possession.

Amulets and incantations were used to ward off evil spirits and demons. In one seventh-century Phoenician amulet we find the following incantation intended to protect a woman in childbirth: "O Flying One, O goddess, O Sasam . . . O god, O Strangler of Lambs. The house I enter you shall not enter, the court I rend you shall not tread."

The ancient Jews absorbed some of the animistic notions of the primitive peoples who lived around them and also developed many legends of their own concerning evil spirits that wield destructive power against human beings. Following are some of the usual and interesting references to demons in the Talmud and Jewish mystical books, and the recipes for avoiding them.

1. Physical characteristics of demons

This passage is found in the Talmud (Chagigah 16a).

> Our rabbis taught: Six things are said concerning demons. With regard to three, they are like ministering angels. With regard to three others, they are like human beings. They are like ministering angels in that they have wings, they fly from one end of the world to the other, and they can hear what goes on behind the curtain of heaven. They are like human

beings in that they eat and drink like humans, they procreate like humans, and they die like human beings.

2. Dwelling place of demons

Here are some of the things the Talmud tells us about demons. Their sporting places are caper bushes and spearworts, where they dwell in groups of sixty; nut trees, where they form in groups of nine; and shady spots on moonlit nights, especially the roofs of houses, under gutters, or near ruins. They also live in cemeteries and toilets (there is a special demon of the privy known in Hebrew as shed shel bet ha-kisse). They are also sometimes found in water, oil, and bread crumbs cast on the ground. They are a threat to any persons or things near them (Talmud Pesachim 3b; Berachot 3a, 62b; Shabbat 67a; Gittin 70a; Chullin 105; Sanhedrin 65a).

3. The most dangerous nights for demons

Especially dangerous are Wednesday night and Saturday night. That is when Agrat bat Machlat, the dancing roof demon, haunts the air with the train of 180,000 messengers of destruction, every one of whom has the power of doing harm (Yalkut Chadash, Keshafim 56). On those nights one should not drink water except out of white vessels and after having recited Psalm 29:3–9 (which mentions "voice of God" seven times) or some other magical formula (Talmud Pesachim 3a).

4. Demons in Jewish tradition

Following is a summary of some of the more well-known demons in the world of Jewish demonology:

Asmodeus (Ashmedai): All of the demons were believed to be under the dominion of a chief called Asmodeus or Ashmedai, a name derived from the Persian aesmadiv ("spirit of anger"). He is described as the king of the demons in Pesachim 110a: "Rabbi Joseph said: 'The demon Joseph told me that Ashmedai the king of the demons is appointed over all pairs.'" Asmodeus is also described in the Talmud (Gittin 8a) as "rising every day from his dwelling place on the mountain to the firmament," where he studies in the Academy on High. As a result of this daily practice, he gains knowledge of the fate of human beings, which oftentimes causes him to act in an enigmatic fashion. For example, while on his way to visit Solomon, Asmodeus weeps upon seeing a wedding party, later explaining that the bridegroom has only a short time to live. Similarly, on the same journey, he sets a drunkard on the right path in order so that he will have a share in the world-to-come.

Azazel: The demons in ancient Israelite lore resembled the demons in other cultures. For example, we learn that demons lived in deserts. In the annual ritual ceremony of purification in the ancient sanctuary, Aaron is told to offer two goats, one to God and the other to Azazel, and the goat was to be sent into the wilderness (Leviticus 16:1–10). Many Bible scholars maintain that Azazel was the name of a wilderness demon.

Dever: In Psalm 91:5–6 we are told: "You need not fear the terror (pachad) of night, the arrow (chetz) that flies by day, the pestilence (dever) that prowls in the dark, the scourge (ketev) that stalks at noon." Bible scholars have found that the Hebrew word dever indicates the demon of pestilence.

Lilith: The female demon Lilith is assigned a central position in Jewish demonology. She is mentioned in Isaiah 34:14 as one of the spirits that will lay waste to the land on the day of vengeance. Lilith is also mentioned several times in the Talmud. For instance, in Eruvin 100b she appears as a female demon with a woman's face and wings. In the Alphabet of Ben Sira (tenth century), Lilith is identified with the first Eve. Created from the earth at the same time as Adam, she was unwilling to give up her equality and therefore disputed with him the manner of their intercourse. Pronouncing God's name, she flew off into the air. Adam asked God to send three angels after her. Locating her at the Red Sea, the angels threatened that if she did not return, a hundred of her sons would die every day. She refused, stating that the very nature of her existence was to harm newborn infants. However, she was forced to swear that whenever she saw the image of the angels in an amulet, she would lose her power over infants. In Jewish mysticism, Lilith has two basic roles: in one she strangles children, and in the other she seduces men, resulting in nocturnal emissions through which she bears a never-ending number of demonic children. Lilith has been identified with the Queen of Sheba, based on a Jewish and Arab legend that the Queen of Sheba was actually a jinni, half-human and half-demon. Over time, it became customary to protect women in childbirth from Lilith's great power by placing amulets over the bed or on all four walls of the room. These amulets often included the words of Psalms 126 and121, and the names of the three angels—Sanvei, Sansanavei, and Samangalaf.

Resheph: Resheph was the Canaanite netherworld god of pestilence. He appears in the Bible but is not specifically said to be a god. In both Deuteronomy 32:24 and Habakkuk 3:5 reshef is a synonym for "pestilence."

5. How to avoid demons

Numerous activities were devised through the ages by which to eradicate and avoid the demons. Such activities included observing the Torah, wearing tefillin, affixing a mezuzah to one's home, and putting on ritual fringes (tzitzit). In addition to various amulets, other methods included: carrying lit torches at night, blowing the ram's horn, biblical readings, wearing the colors red and blue, eating sweet things, keeping a knife on hand, rinsing with running water, keeping one's house clean, and spitting three times.

6. The evil eye

From ancient times well into the modern era many Jews believed that an envious or begrudging glance from someone could work evil upon the person to whom it was directed. According to a talmudic statement in Baba Metzia 107b: "Ninety-nine out of a hundred die of an evil eye." Eventually the evil eye came to be seen as a powerful demonic force. A variety of folk beliefs and customs developed to ameliorate its deleterious effects. Measures taken to avert the evil eye come in two forms. The first is preventative. Since it was believed that the evil eye would be activated by arousing jealousy, it called for self-restraint, such as not praising a good-looking newborn, because babies were thought to be especially susceptible to the evil eye. The other form was counter-active. Once the evil eye was activated and danger imminent, counter-magic would be used to deceive or ultimately defeat it.

Following are some preventative measures to avert the evil eye:

> Veil your beauty and do not show off your riches.
> Tie a red band around the wrist or neck of a newborn.
> Use an outstretched arm.
> Wear a chamsa amulet.
> Never use the term "evil eye" in conversation.
> Never mention the birth date or exact age of a person.

Counteractive measures against the evil eye include:

Hanging interesting objects (e.g., precious stones) between the eyes of an endangered person.

Qualify any praise that you give to an object of beauty or a person with the phrase keyn ayin ha-ra ("may there be no evil eye"), often shortened to keynahora.

CHAPTER 6

Magic

Magic is the art that purports to control or forecast natural events, effects, or forces by invoking the supernatural. In contrast to divination, which only attempts to predict the future, magic professes to influence and change the future for good or bad. Charms, spells, and rituals are often employed to achieve supernatural events and control events in nature.

Interest in magic permeated the ancient Near East. In Egypt, for example, magical beliefs and magic were called upon to ward off dead spirits, demons, scorpions, serpents, and wild beasts. They were also used to protect women in childbirth and to ensure the dying person happiness beyond the grave.

The most complete and detailed list of the various kinds of Israelite practitioners of magic is in Deuteronomy 18:10–11: "Let no one be found among you who consigns his son or daughter to the fire, or who is an augur, a soothsayer, an enchanter or sorcerer, one who casts spells or who consults ghosts or familiar spirits, or one who inquires of the dead."

The Bible prohibits the practice of magic, but biblical law did not eradicate sorcery or magic, as attested by the fact that prophets were constantly condemning magicians and sorcerers. For example, Isaiah (3:2–3), speaking in the name of God, says that all augurs and enchanters will be removed from Jerusalem and Judah. And in Second Chronicles 33:6, King Josiah is described as removing from Judah all of those who divined by a ghost or a familiar spirit.

The biblical prohibition of magic also finds expression in the Talmud. Mishnah 7:7 of Sanhedrin equates magic with idolatry. Shabbat 6:10 denounces magical remedies an Amorite custom. And Sanhedrin 10:1 warns that those who pronounce a magical formula over a wound lose their share in the world-to-come.

This being said, the Talmud mentions a number of persons who engaged in some sort of magic. For example, in Gittin 45a, Rav Nachman's daughters are said to have been experienced in magical procedures and are described as stirring a pot of boiling water with their bare hands. The widow Yochani, a faith healer of Jerusalem, was able to delay a birth by magical means. One of the greatest magicians of them all, Choni Ha-Me'aggel (i.e., Choni the circle-drawer), understood the secret of drawing magic circles. He used this ability to bring about rain in time of drought. Shimon ben Shetach, who sought to eradicate magic, was quoted as saying to him in Ta'anit 19a, "If you were not Choni, whom God loves as a son, I would excommunicate you."

The Talmud does not condemn healing by "white magic" (beneficent magic) except when the means employed are pagan or idolatrous in origin. Many scholars were said to be able to consume men with a glance or reduce them to a heap of bones, but since this magic was regarded as punishment for transgressions the victims committed, it seems to have been permitted.

Biblical verses that contained God's name or spoke of God's power were often used in magic. The Book of Psalms was considered an especially potent book for magical purposes. Perhaps the most popular book on the subject of magic using psalms was the Shimmush Tehillim ("Use of Psalms"). Written in the mid-1500s, its opening line states, "The entire Torah is composed of the names of God, and in consequence it has the property of saving and protecting man." The book quotes a tradition that when a town or city is endangered, it can be saved by reciting in order the psalms whose initial letters spell out its name.

Another work, entitled Sefer Gematriot, lists a series of

biblical verses and their magical use. Some of these verses were recited as found in the Bible, but others were recited in reverse order or with transposed words, or were repeated a given number of times. Sometimes a parchment bearing the words was dissolved in a liquid and then imbibed, or was worn on the person as an amulet. Following are some sample verses as listed in the Sefer Gematriot:

> For a child recently circumcised: "So he blessed them that day saying, 'By you shall Israel invoke blessings, saying: God make you like Ephraim and Manasseh'" (Genesis 48:20).
>
> To drive off evil spirits and demons: Recite the following before going to sleep: "May God bless you and protect you. May God deal kindly and graciously with you. May God bestow favor on you and grant you peace" (Numbers 6:24–26).
>
> To gain a good name: You are fair, my darling, you are fair, with your dove-like eyes. (Song of Songs 6:4–9)
>
> To win credibility in an argument: "Give ear, O heavens, let me speak; let the earth hear the words that I utter. May my speech come down as rain, my speech distill as the dew, like showers on young growth, like droplets on the grass" (Deuteronomy 32:1–2).
>
> To have one's prayer answered: "The Lord passed before him and proclaimed: 'The Lord, the Lord—a God compassionate and gracious, slow to anger, abounding in kindness and faithfulness, extending kindness to the thousandth generation, forgiving iniquity, transgression and sin" (Exodus 34:6).
>
> For a melodious voice: "Then Moses and the Israelites sang this song to God. They said: 'I will sing to God, for God has triumphed gloriously. Horse and driver He has hurled into the sea" (Exodus 15:1)
>
> To strengthen one's voice: "Then Judah went up to him and said, 'Please my lord, let your servant appeal to my lord,

and do not be impatient with your servant, you who are the equal of Pharaoh'" (Genesis 44:18).

To arouse love: "Your ointments yield a sweet fragrance, your name is like finest oil. Therefore do maidens love you" (Song of Songs 1:3).

To maintain peace between husband and wife: "Who is she that comes up from the desert, leaning upon her beloved? Under the apple tree I roused you. It was there your mother conceived you, there she who bore you and conceived you" (Song of Songs 8:5).

To cure sterility: "And if you do obey these rules and observe them carefully, the Lord your God will maintain faithfully for you the covenant that God made an oath with your ancestors" (Deuteronomy 7:12).

To halt menstrual flow: "When she becomes clean of her discharge, she shall count off seven days, and after that she shall be clean" (Leviticus 15:28),

For a fever: "So Moses cried out to God, saying: 'O God, pray heal her'" (Numbers 12:13)

For consumption: "It is a guilt offering. He has incurred guilt before the Lord" (Leviticus 5:19).

For success: "The Lord was with Joseph, and he was a successful man. He stayed in the house of his Egyptian master" (Genesis 39:2).

For profitable trade: "Had not the God of my father, the God of Abraham and the fear of Isaac, been with me, you would have sent me away empty-handed. But God took notice of my plight and the toil of my hands, and God gave judgment last night" (Genesis 31:42).

On beginning a piece of work: "Then all the skilled among those engaged in the work made the tabernacle of ten strips of cloth which they made of fine twisted linen, blue, purple, and crimson yarns. Into these they worked a design of cherubim" (Exodus 36:8).

On entering a new home: "On the first day of the first month you shall set up the Tabernacle of the Tent of Meeting" (Exodus 40:2).

For safety on a journey: "When the Ark was to set out, Moses would say: 'Advance, O Lord. May your enemies be scattered and may your foes run from you.' And when the Ark halted, he would say: 'Return. O God, you who are Israel's myriads of thousands'" (Numbers 10:35–36).

To be saved from imminent danger: "Therefore say to the Israelite people: 'I am the Lord. I will free you from the labors of the Egyptians and deliver you from their slavery. And I will take you to be My people, and I will be your God. And you shall know that I, the Lord, am your God who freed you from the labors of the Egyptians'" (Exodus 6:6–7).

In time of trouble: "O my dove, in the cranny of the rocks, hidden by the cliff, let me see your face, let me hear your voice. For your voice is sweet and your face is attractive" (Song of Songs 2:14).

To cause an enemy to drown: "You made Your wind blow, the sea covered them. They sank like lead in the majestic water" (Exodus 15:10).

To win a war: "The Lord, the Warrior—Lord is His name" (Exodus 15:3).

To be victorious against robbers: "Now the clans of Moab are dismayed, the tribes of Moab, trembling grips them. All the dwellers of Canaan are aghast" (Exodus 15:15).

Against slander: "In Your great triumph, You break Your opponents. You send forth Your fury and it consumes them like straw" (Exodus 15:7).

To calm a raging river: "At the blast of Your nostrils the waters piled up. The floods stood straight like a wall, the deeps froze in the heart of the sea" (Exodus 15:8).

To dispel a hallucination: "Terror and dread descend upon them. Through the might of Your army they are still as stone.

Till Your people cross over, O Lord, till Your people cross over whom You have ransomed" (Exodus 15:16).

For intelligence: "Lover, indeed of all the people, their hallowed are all in Your hand. They followed in Your steps, accepting Your pronouncements. When Moses charged us with the Teaching as the heritage of the congregation of Jacob" (Deuteronomy 33:3–4).

For good health after fasting: "Then will I remember My covenant with Isaac, and also My covenant with Abraham, and I will remember the land" (Leviticus 26:42).

To bring upon another a curse: "No human being who has been proscribed can be ransomed. He shall be put to death" (Leviticus 27:29).

To eradicate evil demons and spirits: "You who dwell in the shelter of the Most High and abide in the protection of Shaddai—I say of God, my refuge, my stronghold. My God in whom I trust, He will save you from the fowler's trap, from the destructive plague. He will cover you with His pinions, and under His wings you shall take refuge. His truth is a shield and armor. You shall not fear the terror by night nor the arrow that flies by day. Of the pestilence that stalks in darkness, nor of the destruction that ravages at noonday. A thousand may fall at your side, and ten thousand at your right hand. But it shall not come near you. You shall behold only with your eyes, and see the recompense of the wicked. Because you have made the Lord your fortress, and the Most High your refuge, no evil shall befall you, neither shall any plague come near your tent. For God will give His angels charge over you, to guard you in all your ways. They shall bear you upon their hands, let you strike your foot against a stone. You shall tread upon the lion and asp, you shall trample on the young lion and serpent. Because he has set his love upon Me, and I will deliver him. I will protect him because he has known My name. He shall call upon Me and I will answer him. I will be with him in trouble, and rescue him and bring him to honor. I will give him abundance of long life, and he shall witness My salvation" (Psalm 91),

Incantations

The incantation was another salient element in Jewish magic. An incantation is the ritual recitation of a charm or spell to produce a magical effect. Most Jewish incantations include an appeal to the ancient masters of magic (e.g., a statement that a magical charm was performed by our teacher Moses on behalf of Joshua), the recitation of biblical passages, the invocation of names of angels, the articulation of holy names, and the mentioning of the actual command. In the Talmud most incantations were read in the name of the mother, and this rule of thumb continued into post-talmudic incantations.

One familiar characteristic of magical incantations is the injunction to do things in reverse, which was believed to be associated with great power when the natural order of things was reversed. This might include saying a verse backward, putting on one's clothing backward, and walking backward.

Following are a couple of sample incantations:

1. To ward off Shabriri

The Talmud (Pesachim 112a) cites an incantation to ward off the demon of blindness, known as Shabriri. In order to eradicate this demon, one must recite the following formula: "My mother told me to beware of shabriri, briri, riri, iri, ri." The idea in this incantation is that as one decreases the letters of the demonic name Shabriri, the demon himself begins to shrink in size and finally vanishes.

2. The mystical abracadabra

The mystical word "abracadabra" is derived from the Aramaic and was often used as a formula of incantation against fever or inflammation. Medieval patients were advised to wear this magic word, written in the following manner, on an amulet, in the belief that it would ward off and cure disease:

```
A B R A C A D A B R A
A B R A C A D A B R
A B R A C A D A B
A B R A C A D A
A B R A C A
A B R A
A B R
A B
A
```

3. Incantation against a fever demon

The following is an incantation quoted by Rabbi Eleazar of Worms in the Middle Ages for eradicating the fever demon: Ochnotinos, chnotinos, notinos, otinos, tinos, inos, nos, os.

Amulets

The amulet (kame'a in Hebrew) was a very popular magical device either worn by a person or attached to an objects or animal. Such magical devices have been created and worn by people from earliest times in an effort to obtain that extra amount of protection from supernatural forces. The custom developed for people to have on their persons pieces of paper, parchment, metal discs, and the like inscribed with formulas that protected the bearer from evil spirits and demons.

Amulets are frequently mentioned in the Talmud. In the Mishnah, amulets are mentioned in Shabbat 6:2 and Shekalim 3:2 as being worn for the curative powers they were believed to possess. The simplest amulet had an inscription of the name of God (often either Yawah or Shaddai) on a piece of parchment or metal.

In the Middle Ages, the rabbinic attitude toward amulets varied. Maimonides strongly opposed them (Guide for the Perplexed 1:61). On the other hand, Nachmanides permitted their use.

Many mystical Jewish texts, including Sefer Yetzira and Sefer Razi'el contain instructions for the preparation of amulets and charms. Three biblical verses (Exodus 14:19–21) were believed to have the highest mystical significance. Since each of the verses consists of seventy-two letters, corresponding to the seventy-two letters of one of the mysterious names of God, they were assumed to represent the ineffable divine name, and were inserted into the amulets in varied forms as an appeal to God for protection.

Following are some examples of amulets as found in Jewish tradition.

Magic triangle: By gradually reducing the size of an inscription, the evil spirit is eased out of its victim and its potency is substantially diminished.

Magic squares and rectangles: These are divided into boxes, each of which contains one or more Hebrew letters. Acrostics can be formed in which powerful inscriptions may be secretly placed in the amulets. The squares vary from those of nine boxes to those of sixty-four or even one hundred boxes. One popular magic square uses the Hebrew letters in Deuteronomy 7:15: "God will take away from you all sickness."

Hexagram: The Star of David, consisting of six points, often contains the Hebrew letters for "Jerusalem" (yerushalayim) or "King David" (melech David). The hexagram symbol also appears in written amulets

The menorah: The seven-branched candelabrum is often found on shiviti amulets from Persia. Shiviti is the first word of Psalm 16:8: "I have set the Lord always before me." In silver amulets only the initial letters of the words are used, but in parchment ones the verses are written out in full. Tradition says that King David's shield was shaped like these silver amulets, and headed with the words "I have set the Lord always before me."

The chamsa: The chamsa, so named from the Arabic word for "five," looks like a hand, often with an eye in the palm. It is used to ward off the power of the evil eye.

Gems

Precious stones and gems have also been used for magical purposes to ward off evil spirits and demons. The Bible (Exodus 28:17–20) speaks of the Urim and Thummim, twelve gems engraved with the tribal names which were attached to the breastplate of the high priest. Used as sacred means of divination, the gems were known for their ability to answer questions on occasions fateful for the Israelite nation.

Here is a summary of several gems that are discussed in Sefer Gematriot:

Odem (Ruby): Connected with Reuben, this stone was used to prevent the woman who wears it from suffering a miscarriage.

Pitdah (Topaz): The stone of Simeon, it is useful to chill the body and in affairs of the heart.

Bareket (Emerald): This is the stone of evil, making people wise and helping to light up their eyes.

Nofech (Carbuncle): This green stone, the stone of Judah, functions to add strength and help attain victory in battle.

Sapir (Sapphire): The stone of Issachar, it is purple-blue in color and is known for its ability to cure ailments.

Yahalom (Emerald): This is the stone of Zebulun, able to bring success in trade and also known for its ability to relieve sleeplessness.

Leshem (Jacinth): The stone of Dan, it allows one's face to be seen.

Shevo (Agate): This is the stone of Naphtali; it prevents stumbling and falling.

Achlama (Amethyst): The stone of Gad, it is useful in war.

Tarshish (Beryl): The stone of Ashur, it is useful for burning up bad food in one's body.

Shoham (Onyx): This is Joseph's stone, bestowing grace upon the bearer and inducing people to listen to what one says.

Yashfe (Jasper): The stone of Benjamin, it has the power to restrain both one's tongue and one's blood.

CHAPTER

7

Medicine and Healing

Ancient Jewish medicine was a combination of science, superstition, and folklore. Supernatural agents were often considered to be the causes of illness and disease, and remedies often included incantations accompanied by other rites and rituals. Following are some rabbinic passages that reflect the many recipes that belong to the category of Jewish folk medicine.

Remedies

1. For a fever

Abaye said: My mother told me that for a daily fever you should take a new zuz coin, go to a salt deposit, take the zuz's weight in salt, and tie the salt inside the collar of your shirt with a band of twined strands of wool. If this remedy does not help, sit at a crossroads, and when you see a large ant carrying something, take it, put it into a brass tube, close the tube's openings with lead, and seal it with sixty seals. Then shake it, lift it on your back, and say to it, "Your burden be upon me, and my burden be upon you." If this remedy does not help, take a new jar, small in size, go to the river, and say to it, "River, lend me a jarful of water for a guest who happens to be visiting me." Circle the jar seven times about your head, then pour its water behind your back and say to it, "River, take back the water you gave me, for the guest who visited me came for a day and left the same day." (Talmud, Shabbat 66b)

2. For tertian fever

Rabbi Huna said: As a remedy for tertian fever, take seven prickles from seven date palms, seven chips from seven beams, seven pegs from seven bridges, seven handfuls of ash from seven ovens, seven pinches of earth from seven graves, seven bits of pitch from seven ships, seven seeds of cumin, and seven hairs from the beard of an old dog, and tie them inside the collar of your shirt with a band of twined strands of wool. (Talmud, Shabbat 67a)

3. For a rash

For a rash, say, "Bazbaziah, Masmasiah, Kaskasiah, Sharlai, and Armarlai"—these are the angels who were sent out from the land of Sodom to heal those smitten with a rash— "Bazakh, Bazikh, Bazbazikh, Masmassikh, Kammon, Kamikh, our color is to remain what it is now, your place is to be confined to where it is now. Like one whose seed is locked up, or like a mule that is not fruitful and cannot increase, so may your seed not be fruitful nor increase in the body of so-and-so son of son-and-so." (Talmud, Shabbat 67a)

4. For epilepsy

Against epilepsy, say, "A sword drawn, a sling stretched, its name is not Yuchav—'sickness and pain.'" (Talmud, Shabbat 67a)

5. For depression

If a person is seized by depression, what is the way to heal him? Red meat broiled over coals, and diluted wine. (Talmud, Gittin 67b)

6. For a migraine headache

For a migraine, take a woodcock and cuts its throat with a white silver coin over the side of the head where the pain is concentrated, taking care that the blood does not blind your eyes. Then hang the bird on your doorpost, so that you can rub against it when you come in and when you exit. (Talmud, Gittin 69a)

7. For cataracts

For a cataract, take a seven-hued scorpion, dry it out in the shade, and mix two parts of ground kohl to one part of ground scorpion; then, with a paintbrush, apply three drops to each eye—no more, lest the eye burst. (Talmud, Gittin 69a)

8. For night blindness

Take a rope made of wool and with it tie one of your own legs to the leg of a dog, and have children rattle potsherds behind you, saying, "Old dog, stupid cock." Collect seven pieces of raw meat from seven houses, place them in a door socket, and then have the dog eat them over the ash pit of the town. After that, untie the rope, and have people say to you, "Blindness of so-and-so son of so-and-so, instead seize the pupils of the dog's eyes." (Talmud, Gittin 69a)

9. To stop a nosebleed

Call a priest whose name is Levi and write "Levi" backward or else call any other man and write backward, "I am Papi Shila bar Sumki," or else write "the taste of the bucket in water of blemish."

If this does not work, take clover roots, the rope of an old bed, papyrus, saffron, and the red part of a palm branch, and burn them all together. Then take a fleece of wool, twine it into wicks, steep them in vinegar, roll them in ashes, and put them into your nostrils. (Talmud, Gittin 69a)

10. To stop mouth bleeding

The blood should be tested by means of wheaten straw. If the straw is softened, the blood comes from the lung and there is a remedy for that. If the straw is not softened, the blood comes from the liver and there is no remedy for that.

If the blood comes from the lung, take seven fistfuls of jujube berry, three fistfuls of lentils, a fistful of cumin, a fistful of string, and a quantity equal to all these of the ileum of a firstborn animal. Then cook the mixture and eat it, washing it down with strong beer made during the month of Tevet. (Talmud, Gittin 69a)

11. For a toothache

Rabbah bar R. Chuna said: Take a whole head of garlic, grind it with oil and salt, and apply it on your thumbnail to the side where the tooth aches. Put a rim of dough around it, taking care that it does not touch your flesh, as it may cause leprosy. (Talmud, Gittin 69a)

12. To restore virility

Abaye said: If you are unsure of your virility, bring three small measures of thorny saffron, pound it, boil it in wine, and drink it. Rabbi Yochanan said: This is exactly what restored me to the vigor of my youth. (Talmud, Gittin 70a)

13. To restore strength to the heart. Abaye said

My mother told me: One who suffers from weakness of the heart should get meat from the right leg of a ram and dried cattle excrement dropped during the month of Nisan. If he has no dried cattle droppings, he should get chips of willow and roast the meat over them. He should then eat it and drink diluted wine. (Talmud, Eruvin 29b)

14. For a scorpion bite

Take the gall of a white stork in beer. This is to be rubbed into the wound, and the rest should be given to the child to drink. A one-year-old stung on his birthday by a wasp is also not likely to live. What is a remedy? The fiber of a date palm soaked in water. This should be rubbed into the wound, and the rest should be given to the child to drink. (Talmud, Ketubot 50a)

15. For a bodily wound

To stop the bleeding, use pepperwort in vinegar. To induce new growth of flesh, take peelings of cynodon and the paring of a thornbush, or worms from a dunghill. (Talmud, Avodah Zarah 28a)

16. For a growth on the eye

Rabbi Safra said: A berry-sized growth on the eye is an emissary of an angel of death. The remedy is run in honey or parsley in an inferior wine. In the meantime, a berry resembling it in size should be brought and rolled over it. A white berry for white growth, and a black berry for a black growth. (Talmud, Avodah Zarah 28a)

17. For a bacterial infection

Rava said: A bacterial infection is a forerunner of a fever. It should be spanned sixty times with the middle finger and then cut open crosswise and lengthwise. This should be done only if its head is not white. If white, it is not dangerous. (Talmud, Avodah Zarah 28a)

18. For an earache

Take the kidney of a hairless goat, cut it crosswise and lengthwise, put it over glowing coals, and pour the water that comes out of it—neither hot or cold, but tepid, into the ear. If this does not work, take the fat of a large scarab beetle, melt it, and let it drip into the ear. (Talmud, Avodah Zarah 28b)

19. For jaundice

Feed the patient the flesh of a donkey. A person bitten by a mad dog should be fed the lobe of its liver. (Talmud, Yoma 84a)

20. For worms in the bowels

Pennyroyal should be eaten with seven black dates. If there are no black dates, swallow with white cress. If that still does not help, fast, then fetch some fat meat, put it over glowing coals, suck out the marrow from a bone, and gulp down vinegar. (Talmud, Shabbat 109b)

21. For a meat bone stuck in the throat

Bring more of that meat, place it on his head, and say, "One by one, go down, swallow; swallow, go down, one by one." If it is a fish bone, say, "You are stuck like a pin, locked up as in a cuirass. Go down, go down." (Talmud, Shabbat 67a)

22. For bad breath

After every food eat salt and after every beverage drink water and you will come to no harm. (Talmud, Berachot 40a)

23. For foot trouble

Plaster your feet with the excrement of cattle. (Song of Songs Rabbah II, 3, 2)

24. For heartburn

Rabbi Chama ben Chaninah said: One who takes black cumin regularly will not suffer heartburn."

CHAPTER 8

Prayer

Prayer is the natural expression of our religious feelings. In the Jewish tradition, prayer has always occupied a position of importance. The Bible records the personal and often spontaneous prayers of the great men and women in the early history of the people of Israel.

The development of congregational worship is a distinct contribution of Judaism to the other faiths that sprang from it. Prayer, especially of the communal variety, continues to be the Jew's way of communicating with God. And the prayerbook continues to define the moral and ethical concepts that lie at the core of Judaism. This chapter will present some unusual and probably surprising facts related to the topic of prayer in the Jewish tradition.

1. The First Reform prayerbook

The first Reform prayerbook appeared in Germany in 1818. The book provided a Hebrew text with German translation and opened on the left, thus underscoring the primacy of German. Keeping true to the theology of Reform Judaism, all references to the ancient Temple service, sacrifices, the Messiah, and the restoration of Israel to Zion were eliminated.

2. Prayer for nullification of a dream

According to the Talmud (Berachot 55b), a person who has a dream and does not remember its content is to stand before the priests at the time when they spread out their hands and say as follows:

> Sovereign of the Universe, I am Yours and my dreams are Yours. I have dreamt a dream and I do not know what it is. Whether I have dreamt about myself or my companions have

dreamt about me, or I have dreamt about others, if they are good dreams, confirm them and reinforce them like the dreams of Joseph. If they require remedy, heal them, as the waters of Marah were healed by Moses our teacher, and as Miriam was healed of her leprosy, and Hezekiah of his sickness, and the waters of Jericho by Elisha. As You did turn the curse of the wicked Balaam into a blessing, so turn all my dreams into something good for me.

He is to conclude his prayer along with the priests, so that the congregation can answer "Amen." If the person cannot manage to finish together with the priests, he should say: "You who are majestic on high, who abides in might, You who are at peace and Your name is peace, may it be Your will to bestow peace on us."

3. Blessing the sun and the moon

Most people would be surprised to know that there is a blessing for the sun and the moon. With regard to the sun, the ancient rabbis taught that a person who sees the sun at its turning point, the moon in its power, the planets in their orbits, or the signs of the zodiac in their order is to recite, "Blessed are You who makes the work of creation." This opportunity occurs only once in every twenty-eight years; or, according to Abaye, when the signs of the zodiac in their orderly progress begin again (Talmud, Berachot 59b).

The blessing of the sun (birkat ha-chammah) is a prayer service in which the sun is praised in thanksgiving for its having been created and set into motion in the firmament on the fourth day of creation. The ceremony takes place after the morning service, when the sun is about 90 degrees above the eastern horizon, on the first Wednesday of the month of

Nisan. It begins with the recitation of Psalms 84:12, 75:5, and 75:2, Malachi 3:20, Psalm 97:6, and Psalm 148. This is followed by the blessing Baruch atah Adonai Eloheynu melech ha-olam oseh ma'aseh vereshit ("Praised are You, Adonai our God, Source of creation"). Next, Psalms 19 and 121 are read, followed by the hymn El Adon. The ritual ends with a thanksgiving prayer in which the community thanks God for sustaining it. The most recent blessings of the sun occurred on April 8, 1953 and March 18, 1981. The next blessing of the sun is scheduled to occur on April 7, 2009!

The blessing of the moon originated in the time of the Second Temple. The basic text for this unusual blessing is presented in the Talmud (Sanhedrin 42 and Soferim 2:1). The prayer can be recited from the third evening after the appearance of the new moon until the fifteenth of the lunar month. The blessing is recited because Judaism sees the moon as a symbol of both the renewal of nature and Israel's renewal and redemption. It is preferable to recite the blessing of the moon in the presence of a minyan of ten persons. The moon must be clearly visible and not obscured by the clouds. Here is the basic text for the blessing of the New Moon:

> Rabbi Yochanan said: Whoever blesses the New Moon at the proper time is considered as having welcomed the presence of the Shechinah. "Halleluyah. Praise God from the heavens. Praise God, angels on high. Praise God, sun and moon and shining stars. Praise God, highest heavens. Let them praise the Name of God, at whose command they were created, at whose command they endure forever, and by whose laws nature abides (Psalm148:1–6).
>
> Praised are You, God, Sovereign of the Universe, whose word created the heavens, whose breath created all that they

contain. God set statutes and seasons for them so that they would not deviate from their assigned tasks. Happily they do the will of their Creator, whose work is truth. God said to the moon that it was to renew itself, a crown of glory for those born from the womb, who are destined to be renewed and to extol their Creator, for the name of God's glorious sovereignty. Praised are You, God, who renews the months.

David, King of Israel, lives and endures.

Greetings are then exchanged with three different people: Shalom aleychem—aleychem shalom.

Then recite three times: May a good sign and may good fortune be ours and blessing for us and for the entire House of Israel. Amen.

4. The shortest prayer in the Bible

In the book of Numbers, Moses offers this short prayer on behalf of his sister Miriam, who has been stricken with the dreaded disease of leprosy: El na refa na lah ("God, please heal her"). There are numerous congregations today that continue to use these words as a healing prayer when they ask people to stand and name persons in need of healing. This is followed by the singing of El Nah.

5. Prayer upon seeing 600,000 or more Jews together

Here is a most unusual blessing that we are enjoined to say if we see 600,000 or more Jews gathered together in one place: Baruch atah Adonai Eloheynu melech ha-olam chacham ha-razim "Praised are You, Adonai Our God, Ruler of the Universe, Knower of secrets."

6. Five once-a-year–only blessings

One of the great prayer-trivia questions of all time is ask someone to name the five blessings that a Jew has only one opportunity per year to say. According to many scholarly Jewish liturgists, the five once-a-year-only blessings are:

Blessing for lighting candles on Yom Kippur: Baruch atah Adonai Eloheynu melech ha-olam asher kiddeshanu be-mitzvotav ve-tzivanu lehadlik ner shel Yom ha-Kippurim: Praised are You, Adonai our God, Ruler of the Universe, who has made us holy by His commandments and commanded us to kindle the lights of the Day of Atonement.

Blessing on seeing blossoms for the first time each year: Baruch atah Adonai Eloheynu melech ha-olam shello chissar be-olamo davar u-vara vo briyot tovot ve-ilanot tovim le-hannot bahem beney adam. Praised are You, Adonai our God, Ruler of the Universe, who has withheld nothing from the world and who has created lovely creatures and beautiful trees for people to enjoy.

Blessing said during the Amidah of the afternoon service on the Ninth of Av: Baruch atah Adonai menachem tziyon u-vone yerushalayim. Praised are You, Adonai, Comforter of Zion and Builder of Jerusalem.

Blessing on searching for chametz: Baruch atah Adonai Eloheynu melech ha-olam asher kiddeshanu be-mitzvotav ve-tzivanu al bi'ur chametz. Praised are You, Adonai our God, Ruler of the Universe, who has made us holy by His mitzvot and commanded us concerning the expulsion of leaven.

Blessing after Barechu prayer on Yom Kippur morning: Baruch atah Adonai Eloheynu melech ha-olam ha-pote'ach lanu sha'arey rachameem u-me'ir eyney ha-mechakim lislichato yotzer or u-vore choshech oseh shalom u-vore et ha-kol. Praised are You, Adonai our God, Ruler of the universe, who opens for us the gates of Your mercy and lightens the eyes of those that hope for Your forgiveness, who forms light and creates darkness, who makes peace and creates everything.

7. Three unusual blessings

It was Rabbi Meir (Talmud, Menachot 43b) who suggested centuries ago that Jews ought to recite one hundred blessings daily, which comes out to one every ten minutes of their life. In this way the Jewish people would be constantly aware of the world around them and respond to it in gratitude. Here are three blessings that are rather unusual and are proof positive that Jewish blessings can relate to almost anything life has in store for us.

On seeing a tree or creature of unusual beauty: Baruch atah Adonai Eloheynu melech ha-olam shekacha lo be-olamo. Praised are You, Adonai our God, Ruler of the Universe, who has such beauty in the world.

On seeing someone of abnormal appearance: Baruch atah Adonai Eloheynu melech ha-olam meshanne ha-briyot. Praised are You, Adonai our God, Ruler of the Universe, who makes people different.

After leaving the bathroom: Baruch atah Adonai Eloheynu melech ha-olam asher yatzar et ha-adam be-chachma u-vara vo nikavim nikavim chalulim chalulim galu'i ve-yadu'a lifney chisse chevodecha she'im yipate'ach echad mehem o yissatem echad mehem ee efshar lehitkayyem ve-la'amod lifanecha. Baruch atah Adonai rofe chol basar u-maflee la'asot. Praised are You, Adonai our God, Ruler of the Universe, who has formed people in wisdom and created in them many orifices and hollow tubes. It is well known that if one of them were to be obstructed or broken, it would be impossible to stay alive. Praised are You, Healer of all flesh, who does wondrous things.

CHAPTER 9

Jewish Education

Known as the People of the Book, Jews have always valued the importance of study and education, which is one of the greatest of all the mitzvot. The original instructors in Bible times were the priests and the Levites, and in later years members of the tribe of Issachar and descendants of Jethro the Kenite. In rabbinic times parents continued to be the purveyors of knowledge to their children. Here are some interesting and unusual facts related to the world of Jewish education.

1. Harvard University and Hebrew

When Harvard College was founded in colonial times, students were required to know Hebrew in order to graduate. In fact, for many years the commencement speeches at Harvard were actually delivered in the Hebrew language!

2. Never on Christmas Eve

Although pious Jews consider themselves obligated to study the Torah and Jewish teachings both day and night, there was one night in the year when they considered the study of the Torah expressly forbidden, and that was Christmas Eve.

3. Maimonides' educational innovations

Many educational practices and ideas that are considered to be of modern origin were actually conceived and practiced by Maimonides eight hundred years ago. Following are some of the educational ideas of Maimonides that are currently practiced and considered modern innovations:

> Individual differences
> Special education for the gifted
> Homogenous grouping

Limiting class size
Employment of visual aids
Incentives to stimulate the learning process
Rapport between teacher and student
Physical education in the curriculum
Mental hygiene programs
Readiness program for preschool children
Testing program
Study of foreign languages in school curriculum

4. Mitzvah of swimming

According to the Talmud (Kiddushin 30b), it is a mitzvah for a father to teach his son a craft, but it is also a mitzvah for a father to teach his son how to swim, because one day his life may depend on it!

5. Teacher respect and proximity

According to the Talmud (Berachot 8a), a person should always live in the same town as his teacher. Moreover, a student is required to light his teacher's way at night by walking in front of him with a torch. A student is also required to help his teacher dress and put on shoes, and to stand by his teacher while he sleeps (Yalkut Shimoni, Beshallach 226).

6. First house of learning

The bet ha-midrash (house of study) is first mentioned in the Wisdom of Ben Sira 51:23 (second-century c.e.) In the Talmud (Baba Batra 21a) mention is made of state-employed teachers in Jerusalem who took care of children from the provinces who lacked the advantage of home instruction. Sometime between the intertestamental period, formal Jewish schools for children were started in the synagogues. By the beginning of the common era, all Jewish children were required to go to school. They learned how to read and write by studying the Bible.

7. Learning classifications for students

Today, school psychologists often classify learning-challenged students in a variety of categories. Centuries ago, the tractate Ethics of the Fathers 5:18 classified students by comparing them to four objects: a sponge, which soaks up everything; a funnel, which takes in at one end and lets out at the other; a strainer, which forfeits the wine and retains the dregs; a sieve, which gives up the bran and retains the fine flour.

CHAPTER **10**

Amazing Jewish Miracles

There is no biblical word for "miracle." The closest related words are "wonder" (mofet) and "sign" (ot). Our ancestors regarded the miracles of the Bible as literally true and authentic. They did not differentiate between the natural and the supernatural, since it was one all-powerful God that caused all to be and set the course of nature according to His will.

Following are some of the more exciting miracle stories that demonstrate the love of God for the Jewish people. They are culled from both the Bible and rabbinic literature.

1. Manna from heaven (Exodus 16:14)

About six weeks after the Israelites escaped from Egypt, when they were not yet accustomed to life in the wilderness, the provisions they had brought with them were exhausted. Soon thereafter there appeared on the ground in the wilderness a fine, scale-like thing, fine as the hoarfrost on the ground. On seeing it, the Israelites asked one another: What is this? (Man hu in Hebrew). They did not know what it was, but Moses explained that it was bread that God had given them to eat. It was like coriander seed, white, and had the taste of wafers made with honey. The manna was miraculously supplied to the Israelites until they entered Canaan and the fruit of the land was available.

2. The healing serpent of brass (Numbers 21:9)

In a most astounding story presented in Numbers 21, the Israelites spoke out against God and Moses, complaining about the miserable food in the wilderness. God sent fiery serpents among the people, many of whom were bitten and died. It was then that the Israelites appealed to Moses, having realized their sin of speaking against God. Moses interceded. Here is the way the Bible tells the rest of the story:

> Then God said to Moses, "Make a fiery figure and mount it on a standard. And if anyone who is bitten looks at it, that person shall recover." Moses made a copper serpent and mounted it on a standard. And when anyone was bitten by a serpent, he would look at the copper serpent and recover.

3. Nebuchadnezzar's furnace rendered harmless (Daniel 3:20)

The first six chapters of the Book of Daniel tell about the miraculous deliverance of the prophet Daniel and his three friends, who had been exiled to Babylon by Nebuchadnezzar before the fall of Judea. These three high-ranking administrators, Shadrach, Mishach, and Abednego, were greatly affected by the decree that King Nebuchadnezzar issued to all the top functionaries, namely, to bow down to the image he had set up. The three ignored the decree, and the king ordered them thrown into a blazing furnace. But not even their clothes were singed. King Nebuchadnezzar was so moved by the miracle he had witnessed with his own eyes that he offered a blessing to God.

4. Daniel and the lions (Daniel 6:16)

In the sixth chapter of the Book of Daniel, Daniel is accused by his rivals of showing disregard for the Persian king, Darius. The king had no choice but to sentence him to death. Daniel was cast into a den of lions. Here is the rest of the story as told in the Bible (Daniel 6:17–23):

The king spoke and said to Daniel: "Your god whom you serve continually, He will deliver you." A stone was brought and laid upon the mouth of the den and the king sealed it with his own signet. Then the king went to his palace, and passed the night fasting, neither were diversions brought before him, and his sleep fled from him. Then the king arose very early in the morning and went in quickly to the den of lions. And when he came near to the den he cried with a pained voice. The king spoke and said to Daniel, "O Daniel, servant of the living God, is your God, whom you serve continually, able to deliver you from the lions?" Then Daniel said to the king: "O king, live forever! My God has sent His angel and has shut the lions' mouths, and they have not hurt me."

5. Test of the staffs (Numbers 17:16–24)

After Korach and his followers tried to wrest the leadership from Moses, they were killed by an earthquake. However, more persuasion was still necessary if all the Israelites were to be thoroughly convinced that Aaron had been chosen to serve as high priest (Numbers 17:16) The test of the staff was created to settle this issue of doubt once and for all. Here is how the Bible (Numbers 17:16–24) tells it:

God spoke to Moses saying: "Speak to the Israelites and take from them, from the chieftains of an ancestral house: twelve staffs in all. Inscribe each person's name on his staff. Also inscribe Aaron's name on the staff of Levi. Deposit them in the Tent of Meeting before the Pact, where I meet you. The staff of the person whom I choose shall sprout, and I will rid myself of the constant complaints of the Israelites against you." The next day Moses entered the Tent of the Pact, and there the staff of Aaron and the house of Levi had sprouted.

It had brought forth sprouts, produced blossoms, and borne almonds.

6. The cloud of glory (Exodus 13:21–22)

After the splitting of the Sea of Reeds and the Israelites passage through, the Bible informs us that God was with them by day in a pillar of cloud, to lead the way, and by night in a pillar of fire, to give them light. The cloud has come to be understood as God's messenger and a manifestation of God's mercy and divine protection.

7. The sun and the moon stood still (Joshua 10:12)

In another celestial miracle, the Book of Joshua tells how the sun and the moon were made to stop for one day so that the Israelites could win a victory over their enemies. Here is the miracle in the Bible's own words:

> Then Joshua spoke to God in the day when God delivered the Amorites before the children of Israel. And he said in the sight of Israel: "Sun, stand still upon Gibeon. And you moon, in the valley of Aijalon." And the sun stood still and the moon stayed.

Miracle Stories About Elijah

The prophet Elijah, who lived in the ninth century C.E., has been described as the most romantic and enigmatic character in the whole range of Jewish history. He is the leading man in innumerable Jewish folklore tales and has been credited with countless miraculous deeds. Here are some of them.

1. Elijah and the widow (I Kings 17:9-16)

In the First Book of Kings, Elijah makes his initial appearance on the scene with great suddenness. As with Moses, little is told of his earlier life. There was once a drought in Israel, and the word of God came to Elijah as follows:

> "Arise, go to Zarephat, which belongs to Zidon, and dwell there. Behold, I have commanded a widow who lives there to sustain you." So Elijah arose and went to Zerephat, and when he came to the city gate, a widow was there gathering sticks.
>
> He called to her and said: "Fetch me a little water in a vessel, that I may drink." And as she was about to bring it, he called to her and said: "Bring me a morsel of bread in your hand." And she said: "As the Lord your God lives, I do not have any cake, only a handful of meal in a jar, and a little oil in a cruse, and behold, I am gathering two sticks, that I may go in and dress it for me and my son, that we may eat it, and die." And Elijah said to her: "Do not be afraid. Go and do as you have said, and afterward make for you and for your son. For thus says the God of Israel: 'The jar of meal shall not be spent, neither shall the cruse of oil fail, until the day that God sends rain upon the land.'"
>
> And she went and did according to the saying of Elijah, and she, and her house, did eat many days, neither the oil fail, according to the word of God, which God spoke to Elijah.

2. Elijah obtains rain (I Kings 18:41)

In the time of King Ahab, the Israelites were wavering between God and Baal. Ahab was a generous ruler, but weak-willed and dominated by his Phoenician wife, Jezebel. It was high treason to proclaim the God of Israel, and once again the figure of Elijah stands out in greatness. At the end of chapter 18 of the First Book of Kings, a drought has settled upon the land. Here is how the Bible (I Kings 18:42–45) tells the story:

> Elijah went to the top of Mount Carmel and bowed himself down upon the earth, putting his face between his knees. And he said to his servant: "Go up now, look toward the sea." And he went up and looked and said, "There is nothing." And he said: "Go again seven times." And it came to pass at the seventh time, that he said: "Behold, there arises a cloud out of the sea, as small as a man's hand." And he said: "Go up, say to Ahab: 'Make ready your chariot, and get down, that the rain does not stop you.'" And it happened in a short while that the heaven grew black with clouds and wind, and there was a great rain.

3. Descent of fire on Mount Carmel (I Kings 18:38)

In chapter 18 of the First Book of Kings, Elijah meets and confronts King Ahab and his Phoenician wife, Queen Jezebel. In those days it was high treason to proclaim the God of Israel. Both the king and the queen permitted the worship of the pagan god Baal. Against this dark setting, Elijah fearlessly pronounced the doom that would follow upon their apostasy and their outrage of justice.

Elijah the prophet challenged King Ahab and Queen Jezebel for their Baal worship, asking the Baal priests to come to Mount Carmel, where he would demonstrate who the true God really was. Two altars were constructed on Mount Carmel. When the false priests offered sacrifices to Baal, the sacrifices were not consumed. Elijah then brought a sacrifice to God, which was miraculously burned in answer to Elijah's prayer. The people then proclaimed God to be the One and only One in an overwhelming act of surrender.

4. Splitting the waters of the Jordan (II Kings 2:1–15)

In this story Elijah paid a farewell visit to Jericho and Beth El, centers of the sons of the prophets. He found himself alone with Elisha standing by the Jordan River, with fifty men of the sons of the prophets as eyewitnesses. Elijah took his mantle, wrapped it together, and struck the water, which miraculously divided to the right and to the left, allowing them to cross over onto dry land. Later, after Elijah ascended to heaven in a whirlwind, Elisha picked up Elijah's mantle and returned to the banks of the Jordan. Again, the waters parted to the right and to the left, and Elisha crossed over. When the disciples of the prophets at Jericho saw him from a distance, they exclaimed, "The spirit of Elijah has settled on Elisha."

5. Cake baked on hot stones and the cruse of water (I Kings 19:1–8)

In this incredibly exciting story, Elijah fled from Queen Jezebel's vengeance. Running for his life, he arrived in Beersheba, a place where he believed he would be safe from Jezebel's wrath. Seeing the powerful influence that Jezebel still exercised despite his triumph on Mount Carmel, Elijah lost hope of ever reforming King Ahab and the people. So he prayed for a release from his troubles and the anxieties of an evil world. Lying down under a tree, he went to sleep. Here is the continuation of the story in the words of the Bible:

> An angel touched him, and said to him: "Arise and eat." And he looked, and behold, there was at his head a cake baked on the hot stones, and a cruse of water. He ate and drank, and laid himself down again. And the angel of God came again a second time, and touched him and said: "Arise and eat, be-

cause your journey is too great for you." And he arose and did eat and drink, and went on the strength of that meal forty days and forty nights in Horeb, the mountain of God.

In this miracle story, Elijah was provided by God's angel with food that sustained him for a remarkable period of forty days and nights! This is reminiscent of how Moses, when atop Mount Sinai, likewise lived without food for the same number of days and nights (Exodus 24:8).

6. Feeding by ravens (I Kings 17:6)

In this miracle story, Elijah warned King Ahab that according to the word of God there would be a drought. God then told Elijah to turn eastward and hide by the brook of Cherith, a tributary of the Jordan River. It was there that God told Elijah to drink the water and that the ravens would feed him. And so it was that ravens brought Elijah bread and meat both in the morning and in the evening.

7. Ascent to heaven in a whirlwind (II Kings 2:9–11)

The miraculous ascension of Elijah in a whirlwind is graphically portrayed in the second chapter of II Kings:

> And it came to pass when they were gone over, that Elijah said to Elisha: "Ask what I shall do for you, before I am taken from you." And Elisha said: "I pray you, let a double portion of your spirit be upon me." And he said, "You have requested a difficult thing. Nevertheless, if you see me when I am taken from you, it shall be so to you. But if not, it shall not be so." And it happened, as they still went on, and talked, that there appeared a chariot of fire, and horses of fire, which parted

them both asunder. And Elijah went up by a whirlwind to heaven.

The deep impression left by Elijah's wondrous ascent to heaven made Elijah a legendary figure both in biblical times and in modern times too. Because the Bible does not speak of his actual death, Elijah's presence and spirit continue to flourish in many life-cycle events and rituals, including the circumcision (Chair of Elijah), the Passover Seder (Elijah's cup), and the Havdalah ceremony at the conclusion of the Sabbath, when the hymn Eliyahu Ha-Navi ("Elijah the Prophet") is traditionally sung.

Miracle Stories About Elisha

1. The waters of Jericho (II Kings 2:19–22)

After Elisha was recognized the successor of Elijah, the men of Jericho told him about the problem they were having with bad water. The water caused frequent miscarriages by women and made trees shed their fruits before they were ripe.

And Elisha said: "Bring me a new cruse, and put salt therein." And they brought it to him, and he went forth to the spring of the waters, and threw salt therein. Then he said: "Thus says God: I have healed these waters, there shall not be from thence any more death or miscarrying." So the waters were healed unto this day, according to the word of Elisha which he spoke.

2. The youths and the bears (II Kings 2:23–24)

In the very next Elisha miracle story after the healing of the Jericho waters, Elisha went to Beth El, where the local children mocked him because of his baldness. Elisha cursed them in God's name. Because of the curse, two she-bears emerged from the woods and killed forty-two of the children.

3. Filling the trenches with water without wind or rain (II Kings 3:20)

In this story regarding Israel's preparations for an attack on Moab, a lack of water for his army induced the king of Israel to ask Elisha for help. God's hand came upon Elisha and told him to dig trenches in the valley in which to collect the water that would miraculously flow into them. God further told Elisha that although there would be no rain or wind, the valley would be filled with water, enough for both people and animals.

After the country had been filled with this miraculous water, the Moabites gathered themselves to fight against Israel. Another amazing occurrence took place:

> They rose up early in the morning and the sun shone upon the water, and the Moabites saw the water come from way off as red as blood. And they said: "This is blood: the kings have surely fought together, and they have killed each person his fellow person. Now therefore, Moab, to the spoil." And when they came to the camp of Israel, the Israelites rose up and killed the Moabites, so that they fled.

It appears that since there had been no rain in the land near Moab, the Moabites thought that the valley was dry and naturally imagined it to be full of blood. Thinking that the kings must have fought among themselves and killed each other, they entered the Israelite camp believing that it would be easy to capture it. Much to their surprise, they were ambushed by the Israelites.

4. The pot of oil (II Kings 4:1–7)

The prophet Elisha sought every opportunity to practice loving-kindness and to bring relief and blessing wherever he went in the course of his ministry. In the beginning of the fourth chapter of the Second Book of Kings, we are presented with the following miracle story. A certain woman (commentators have identified her with the widow of Obadiah, the God-fearing minister of King Ahab, who had sheltered the prophets when Jezebel persecuted them) incurred a severe debt that could not be repaid. As a result, her children were to be enslaved in payment. It is here that Elisha came to the rescue:

> Elisha said to her: "What shall I do for you? Tell me, what do you have in your house?" And she answered, "Your handmaid has not anything except for a pot of oil." Then Elisha said: "Go, borrow vessels from neighbors, even empty ones. Go inside, shut the door upon you and your sons, and pour out into all those vessels. And you shall set aside that which is full." So she went from him, shut the door upon her and her sons. They brought the vessels to her, and she poured them out. And it happened that when the vessels were full that she said to her son: "Bring me yet a vessel." And he said to her, "There are no more." And the oil stayed. Then she came and told the man of God. And he said, "Go and sell the oil and pay the debt and you and your children can live on the rest."

5. The bitter pottage of the sons of the prophets (II Kings 4:38–41)

When Elisha came to Gilgal, there was a famine in the land. Elisha instructed his students to cook pottage for the sons of the prophets. One went out into the field to gather herbs. He found a wild vine and gathered wild gourds and shredded them all together in a pot. As they were eating, the bitter taste must have aroused the thought that they were being poisoned, and they told Elisha that "there was death in the pot." Elisha then told them to bring some meal. He cast it into the pot and the mixture in the pot was again edible.

After this occurrence, a man from Baalshalisha brought Elisha bread of the first fruits, twenty loaves of barley and some fresh ears of corn. When told by Elisha to give it to the people to eat, his servant wondered how this small amount of food could feed one hundred men. However, miraculously there was enough. Either the quantity of bread had mysteriously increased or a fifth of a loaf more than satisfied the hunger of each man.

6. Naaman's Leprosy (II Kings 5:1–14)

In this extraordinary episode, Naaman, captain of the host of the king of Aram, was stricken with leprosy and advised to go to Elisha for a cure. Elisha sent a messenger advising him to immerse himself in the Jordan. But Naaman angrily replied, "Are not Aman and Phrapar the rivers of Damascus better than all the waters in Israel?" Subsequently convinced to return to the Jordan River, he immersed seven times according to Elisha's instructions and emerged cured of his leprosy. He then converted to the God of Israel and renounced all other gods, saying: "Behold, now I know that there is no God in all of the earth but in Israel."

7. The floating ax head (II Kings 6:1–7)

In this story, the sons of the prophets wished to dwell near the Jordan River. When they got there, they cut down trees, but accidentally the ax head fell into the water. The one who dropped it was very upset because it had been borrowed. When Elisha learned what had happened, he told the person to cut down a stick and throw it in, and this made the ax head float. He was able to reach out and retrieve it. This wondrous miracle consisted of the fact that when the stick was thrown into the water, it penetrated the hole in the ax head and kept it afloat.

8. Restoration of sight to the blind (II Kings 6:18–20)

In this miracle story, an Aramean army detachment was sent to capture Elisha and was itself entrapped. Here is the story in the Bible's own words:

> When they came down to him, Elisha prayed to God, and said: "Smite the people with blindness." And God smote them with blindness, according to the word of Elisha. And Elisha said to them: "This is not the way, neither is this the city. Follow me and I will bring you to the man whom you seek." And he led them to Samaria. And it came to pass that when they came to Samaria Elisha said: "Open the eyes of these men, that they may again see." And God opened their eyes, and they saw, and behold, they were in the midst of Samaria.

9. Resurrection of a dead man (II Kings 13:21)

In Elisha's last hours, he fell very sick. His courage and amazing spirit passed in one final effort to stimulate resistance to Syria. He instructed King Joash to perform a symbolic act with bow and arrows to ensure victory. However, the king failed to carry it out properly. As a result, Elisha the patriot died with misgiving about the future of the country. Then came the miracle of all miracles:

Now the bands of Moabites used to invade the land at the coming of each year. Once a man was being buried when the people caught sight of such a band, so they threw the corpse into Elisha's grave and went away. When the dead man came into contact with Elisha's bones, he came to life and stood up.

Thus Elisha life ended with the crowning miracle of his career, the revival and resurrection of a dead man!

Miracle Stories in Rabbinic Writings

There are many amazing stories and tales about miraculous occurrences in the writings of the sages. Following is a selection of believe-it-or-not texts from rabbinic writings:

1. Wings of the dove

The gentile government once decreed that anyone who wore tefillin would be punished by having his head broken. Elisha wore them on the street, and when an official ran toward him, he removed his tefillin and placed them in his hands.

"What is that in your hands?" the official asked.

"A pair of pigeon's wings," Elisha replied. He opened his hands and a pair of wings lay there.

Elisha bore in mind the words of the psalmist (Psalm 68:14): "The wings of the dove are covered with silver." As the dove is protected by her own silver wings, so are the children of Israel protected by their mitzvot. (Talmud, Shabbat 19)

2. Miracle of the gold coins

A student of Rabbi Shimon ben Yochai departed for a foreign country where he grew rich. When he returned, the other disciples were jealous and also wished to leave Palestine.

Their master said: "Come with me. I shall work a miracle for you, and the valley here shall be filled with gold coins. But know of a truth that you will have your reward either in the world or in the everlasting life. Make your choice." (Exodus Rabbah 52)

3. The golden table leg

The wife of Rabbi Chanina ben Dosa could not endure their poverty and asked her husband to pray for help. A golden table leg appeared in the room. Later, the rabbi's wife dreamed that she was in paradise. All of the righteous sages there had homes with furniture of gold. Her husband's table, however, was missing a leg. When the rabbi's wife awakened, she begged him to return the golden table leg. (Talmud, Ta'anit 2)

4. Rabbi Chanina ben Dosa

Rabbi Chanina ben Dosa was carrying some salt when it began raining. He said in prayer: "Everyone else feels good, but Chanina does not." The rain stopped. Entering his home he said: "Everyone feels bad except Rabbi Chanina." The rain came down again.

Rabbi Chanina entered his home and discovered his daughter in tears. In error she had poured vinegar into the lamp on the eve of the Sabbath. He declared: "May the One who commanded the oil to burn also command the vinegar to burn." The vinegar burned all day until after Havdalah.

Rabbi Chanina had some goats and was told that they were damaging people's property. He said: "If they really do damage, may bears devour them, but if not, may they bring the bears impaled in their horns." In the evening each of the goats brought a bear on its horns. (Talmud, Ta'anit 24b)

5. The Rip Van Winkle of the Talmud

Rabbi Yochanan said: "All his life this righteous Choni was troubled about the verse 'When God brought back those that returned to Zion, we were like unto them that dream' (Psalm 126:1). Did anyone ever sleep seventy years nonstop?"

One day, while walking on the road, Choni noticed a man planting a carob tree. Choni said to the man: "You know that it takes seventy years before a carob tree yields fruit. Are you certain that you will live seventy years and eat from it?" "I found this world provided with carob trees," the man replied. "As my ancestors planted for me, so I plant for my children."

Thereupon Choni sat down to eat and was overcome by sleep. As he slept, a grotto was formed around him, so that he was screened over from humanity, and thus he slept seventy years. When he awoke he saw a man gathering carobs from the carob tree and eating them. "Do you know who planted this carob tree?" Choni asked. "My grandfather," the man replied. "I must have slept seventy years!" Choni explained. He then went to his home and asked whether the son of Choni the circle maker was still alive. "I am Choni," he said, but the people did not believe him. He took himself to the bet ha-midrash where he heard the scholars say, "Our studies are as clear to us today as they used to be in the times of Choni the circle maker, for when he came to the bet ha-midrash he used to explain to the scholars all of their difficulties."

He said to them: "I am Choni," but they did not believe him, nor did they show him the respect due to him. He therefore prayed for death and did indeed die. (Talmud, Ta'anit 23a)

6. Miraculous breasts

Our rabbis taught: It once happened that a man's wife died and left a child to be suckled, and he could not afford to pay a wet-nurse. Whereupon a miracle occurred and his nipples opened like the two nipples of a woman and he suckled his son. Rabbi Joseph observed, "Come and see how great was this man, that such a miracle was performed on his account." Abaye said to him, "On the contrary, how lowly was this man, that the order of creation was changed on his account." (Talmud, Shabbat 53b)

7. The ark that took up no space

Rabbi Levi said: We have a tradition from our ancestors that the ark took up no room. It has been taught to the same effect: The ark which Moses made had round about it an empty space of ten cubits on every side. Now it is written, "And in front of the sanctuary was twenty cubits in length and twenty in breadth" (I Kings 6:20). It is also written, "And the wing of the one cherub was ten cubits and the wing of the other cherub was ten cubits" (I Kings 6:24). Where then was the ark itself? We must therefore conclude that it stood by a miracle (without taking up any room). (Talmud, Megillah 10b)

8. The well in the wilderness

The well that was with the Israelites in the wilderness had amazing properties. It resembled a rock the size of a beehive, from which, as out of a narrow jug, water coming out in a trickle shot high up into the air like a geyser. The well rolled up the mountains with Israel and went down into the valleys with them. It branched into streams so large that the Israelites would seat themselves in small boats and go visiting one another. (Tosefta, Sukkot 3:11–13; Numbers Rabbah 1:2)

9. The extended day

Rabbi Nehemiah said in the name of Rabbi Mana: "Miracles occurred on that day. It was the eve of the Sabbath, and the inhabitants of all the cities assembled for the mourning over Rabbi Judah the Prince. They set his body down in eighteen synagogues and then conveyed him to Bet She'arim. The day was extended for them so that each Israelite had time to arrive home, kindle the Sabbath light, roast the fish, and fill the cask with water before the Sabbath. When the last of them had done this, the sun set and the rooster crowed. The people began to cry out: "Woe, we have desecrated the Sabbath." A heavenly voice issued forth saying: "Whoever did not stint himself in mourning for Rabbi is destined for the life of the world-to-come, with the exception of Kazra, who was there but did not accompany the funeral procession." On hearing this, the man went up and threw himself from the roof and killed himself by the fall. A heavenly voice went forth and said: "Also Kazra, for what he did on the roof, is destined for the life of the world-to-come." (Ecclesiastes Rabbah 9:3)

CHAPTER 11

Origins

1. Jews and Chinese food

Many Jews truly enjoy Chinese food. Over the years quite a number of kosher Chinese restaurants have been opened to meet the needs of Jews who keep the Jewish dietary laws. Not surprisingly, there are several theories as to why Jews are attracted to Chinese food. One theory is called the "wonton-kreplach" connection. It posits that there are many similarities between Jewish and Chinese food. For one, the Chinese wonton dumpling looks very much like the Jewish dumpling called a kreplach. In addition, Chinese culture has many of the same values as the Jewish tradition: strong emphasis on family, education, productivity and achievement, and devotion to the group. And there has been a lot of wandering and a diaspora for both groups.

An especially intriguing theory is presented in an article entitled "Safe Treif: New York Jews and Chinese Food" written by Gay Tuckman and Harry G. Levine. According to the article, Jews like Chinese food for the same reasons given by people all over the world. It is available, good tasting, and relatively inexpensive. In short, quality, price, and proximity are some of the reasons Chinese food became so important to New York Jews. But these factors appeal to anyone who eats out in a restaurant. There was certainly other restaurant food for New York City Jews to eat, including their own East European foods.

To answer this question, Tuckman and Levine cite several themes in Chinese food that relate to the identity of modern Jews. First, Chinese food is unkosher, and therefore non-Jewish. But because of the specific ways Chinese food is prepared and served, immigrant Jews and their children found it to be more attractive and less threatening than other non-Jewish unkosher food. For example, Chinese food does not mix milk and meat (a practice forbidden by Jewish law), and Chinese restaurant food also uses ingredients that were familiar to East European Jews: chicken, garlic, celery, and onions. In addition, with regard to the nonkosher meat and fish often used in Chinese food, Chinese cooking disguises them by cutting and finely chopping them, so that they look less repulsive.

Second, Jews understood restaurant food as cosmopolitan. Eating in a Chinese restaurant signified that one was not a hick or a greenhorn, but rather that Chinese food was sophisticated in preparation. In other words, it "looked good" to be eating Chinese food, demonstrating a sophisticated palate.

Third, by the second and third generations, Jews identified eating Chinese food as something modern American Jews did together. In other words, it became a Jewish communal custom when eating out to frequent Chinese restaurants. Thus eating Chinese became a New York Jewish custom, a part of daily life, that over time spread to other cities and towns across the country.

2. Jewish-sounding last names

People often ask why Jews have Jewish-sounding last names. To answer this question, let's remember that at the beginning of the biblical period, Jews, then known as Israelites, had no surnames. Men were simply known as Abraham, Isaac, Jacob, and Moses. As the patriarchal families swelled into tribes, more definite identification was necessary, and so-called patronymics came into use. Thus we find Joshua the son of Nun and Caleb the son of Yefuneh. Places of origin began to be used in talmudic times: Nachum the Mede or Hillel the Babylonian.

In the tenth and eleventh centuries, family names became common among Jews and non-Jews. With the rise of cities it became impossible for individuals to know one another as they did in villages and a personal name no longer sufficed. The increase in commerce necessitated a more exact system of naming.

In a number of countries, family names were often derived from Hebrew words, and thus was born the "Jewish-sounding" last name. An occupation often served as the source of a family name. Thus for example, Chazzan is a family naming meaning "cantor," Metzger means "butcher," and Schneider means "tailor."

Other names related to the lineage of a Jewish family. For instance, the last name Cohen or Kahn is usually an indication of priestly lineage, and Levy and Levine indicate a levitical lineage.

As Jews began to assimilate into American society in the twentieth century, it became quite common for families to change surnames that had many syllables into shorter names that would more easily blend into the general society. So, for example, Goldstein became Gold, Levinsky became Levine, Feinberg became Fine, Kaganoff became Kagan.

3. The People of the Book

You may be quite surprised to find out that Muhammad, the Arab founder of Islam, is the person credited with naming the Jews "People of the Book," or in Hebrew, Am ha-Sefer. Muhammad was impressed by the Jewish Bible and felt certain that the people who had produced the Holy Scriptures must have qualities of greatness.

From the days of Ezra the Prophet, the Torah and the

books added to it were so intimately a part of the Jewish people that they could not easily conceive of another way of life. They were aware that acceptance of the Book marked the birth of the Hebrew people. Without continued contact with the Book, the Jews instinctively knew, they could not attain self-fulfillment, or even survive as a people. It was a non-Jew, Muhammad, then, who made explicit a concept they had long lived implicitly.

4. Chinese Jews

Hard as it is to believe, there were and are Chinese Jews, but we usually do not hear much about them. More than 4,500 miles from Israel, a Jewish community of ten thousand people grew up in central China during the Sung Dynasty in the tenth to thirteen centuries. In 1163 this community built a synagogue. As the Sung Dynasty declined, a thousand Jews settled in the city of Kaifeng. In the late 1200s the Kaifeng synagogue was destroyed in a flood and thereafter the community fell into rapid decay. By the middle of the nineteenth century, the Kaifeng Jews preserved only rudimentary knowledge of Judaism, and only the ruins of the former synagogue were left. By the end of World War II, there were only two hundred or so traceable descendants of the original Kaifeng Jewish community.

There are many reasons posited for the assimilation of the Jews of China, including lack of rabbis, lack of a translation of the Torah into Chinese, loss of the Hebrew language over the years, and several destructions of the synagogue from flooding. No new Jewish communities were formed in China until the middle of the nineteenth century. Jews settled in China in the 1840s when Hong Kong was ceded to Great

Britain and foreign concessions were established in Shanghai, Tientsin, and other cities. By 1937 there were about ten thousand Jews living in China.

Hitler caused the greatest influx of Jews to China. Nearly twenty thousand victims of Nazism found a precarious shelter in Japanese-occupied Shanghai from 1938 to 1941. Since 1948 more than a thousand Jews from China have immigrated to the State of Israel.

Today, China's Jewish community numbers around two hundred, nearly all in Shanghai. Led by a Chabad Lubavtich rabbi, Shalom Greenberg, efforts are under way to revive the small Jewish community.

5. Black Jews: Are they for real?

The emergence of Judaism among people of African descent in the first half of the twentieth century is said to have been made possible by a combination of factors. One was a strong religious tradition in the background of the person who became Jewish, embodying Jewish practices from an early but unclear source. When interviewed, many of the older members of the black Jewish community recalled memories of their parents observing certain dietary laws, such as abstaining from pork. Others recalled traditions related to Sabbath or festival observance. In most cases, these practices were fragmentary and observed by people who simultaneously practiced Christianity.

The possible origins of these Hebraic traditions can be traced to West Africa, where a number of tribes have customs so similar to those of Judaism that an ancient connection or maybe even descent from one of the Ten Lost Tribes is conjectured. Another possibility for these well-documented practices is association with Jewish slave owners and merchants in the Caribbean and North America.

Many African Americans who practice Judaism maintain that they have always had a close affinity with the Hebrews of the Old Testament. Scholars such as Albert Raboteau, in his book Slave Religion, have described how the biblical struggle of the Hebrew people, particularly their slavery and exodus from Egypt, bore a strong similarity to the conditions of African slaves and was therefore of special importance to them.

In 1965 a group predominantly comprising young adult black Jews was organized, calling itself Ha-Tza'ad Ha-Rishon ("first step"). In addition to promoting contact between white and black Jews, this group seeks to enlarge Jewish educational opportunities for black Jews.

According to the Encyclopaedia Judaica, no reliable statistics exist for the number of black Jewish congregations or for total membership, but estimates suggest that there are a few dozen groups in New York, Chicago, Philadelphia, Boston, and Cincinnati, with membership between two thousand and six thousand. Most of these groups consist of individuals who have attached themselves to a charismatic figure who claims to have rediscovered the lost roots of the black nation in Judaism. These groups bear such names as Bnei Israel, Temple of the Gospel of the Kingdom, and Kahal Beth B'nai Yisrael. Their knowledge of Hebrew, ritual, and the Bible is very rudimentary.

6. Oriental Jews

The Oriental Jewish communities of the State of Israel originated in various Muslim and Arab-speaking countries, including Yemen, Iraq, Kurdistan (in northern Iraq), Persia (Iran), Afghanistan, and Cochin (in southern India). All of these Oriental Jews have established communities throughout Israel, having fled there in the 1950s because of discrimination and national oppression in their home communities. Today, more than 50 percent of Israel's Jewish population is Oriental.

Each of the Oriental Jewish groups has its own customs and traditions. One of the wildest is the Kurdistan Jewish custom on the last day of Hanukkah. They make a doll that is nicknamed Hanukkah and dress it to look like King Antiochus. They throw the doll into a fire and burn it on the eighth day of Hanukkah each year.

7. Ashkenazic and Sephardic Jews.

The term Ashkenazim generally refers to Jews of European origin or ancestry, while Sephardim generally refers to Jews whose ancestry goes back to Spain, Portugal, or the Arab world. Sephardic communities today are found principally in Turkey, Greece, North Africa, Israel, England, Latin America, and the United States. Ironically, a Jew whose name is Ashkenazi is almost certainly a Sephardic Jew.

It has been estimated that worldwide some 80 percent of all Jews are Ashkenazim, and only 20 percent Sephardim. In Israel, however, more than half of the Jewish population is Sephardic.

One obvious difference between Sephardim and Ashkenazim is in their pronunciation of Hebrew and the liturgy. For example, the Sabbath is pronounced Shabbat in Sephardic, Shabbos by Ashkenazim. The Sephardim claim that their pronunciation of Hebrew and their liturgy are derived from the period of the geonim, who led the great academies of Babylonia until the center of Jewish life shifted to Spain. The text of their prayerbooks is based on the siddur of the distinguished Babylonian gaon, Amram.

The order of prayers, the customs, and the traditions of the Sephardic Jews are known as Minhag Sepharad, as distinguished from Minhag Ashkenaz. Examples of Sephardic customs are:

> Naming a child after a living parent or grandparent, unlike the Ashkenazim, who name after the deceased.
>
> Reciting the Kol Nidre prayer in the manner of a simple prayer; among Ashkenazim, the cantor chants it aloud, and the congregation listens.
>
> Storing the Torah in a hard wood case and reading it upright, whereas Ashkenazim keep the scroll in a soft fabric cover and read it lying flat on a table
>
> At weddings, a Sephardic couple stand together wrapped in a tallit, whereas Ashkenazic couples stand separately
>
> Sephardic Jews call the yearly anniversary of a loved one años, while Ashkenazic Jews use the word yahrzeit
>
> Like the Yiddish-speaking Ashkenazic Jews, Sephardic Jews speak a group language or vernacular known as Ladino. It is written in Hebrew characters and consists primarily of Castilian Spanish mixed with many Hebrew idioms and expressions. It is also studded with Turkish, Arabic, and Greek words.

8. Is it potato kugel or potato kigel?

All languages have dialects and variations in the pronunciation of words. One of the most obvious differences between Ashkenazic and Sephardic Jews is their pronunciation of Hebrew. As exemplified by the words Shabbat and Shabbos, the pronunciation has to do with their dialects. In Ashkenazic dialect, the Sabbath is "Shabbos" because the Hebrew letter tav without a dot in it is pronounced as an s. In the Sephardic dialect, which is used today in modern spoken Hebrew in the State of Israel, the Sabbath is "Shabbat." Because of the t and s variation, a girl who has become a Jewish woman is either a Bas Mitzvah or a Bat Mitzvah, depending on the dialect.

Aside from the Ashkenazic/Sephardic variants of Hebrew, there are also variants in Yiddish depending on where a person was born in Eastern Europe. This is the cause, for instance, of the variation in whether a potato pudding is called a kugel or a kigel. It all depends on whether the speaker is from Poland, Russia, or some other East European country.

The good news is that most people who use one form of a word in spoken language have little trouble being understood by a person using another dialect.

9. Kabbalists and Kabbalah

The Hebrew word kabbalah means "tradition" or "receiving." It designates the mystical teachings of Judaism, originally handed down from generation to generation. The mystical philosophy of kabbalah is hidden and unintelligible to those who have not been properly prepared and instructed in its secret wisdom.

The subjects treated by the kabbalah concern the essence of God, the origin of the universe, the creation of man, the destiny of man and the universe, and the significance of the sacred Torah.

Kabbalah took hundreds of years to develop into a mature mystical teaching. Its origins can be traced to the inner life of the Essenes, a mystical brotherhood of about four thousand people who flourished during Second Temple times. They were ascetics who preferred silence, wore white clothes, and prayed together.

First handed down orally to a chosen few and then committed to writing, the mystical interpretation of the Torah is principally embodied in a work known as the Zohar ("Brightness"), which made its appearance for the first time in thirteenth-century Spain.

Because kabbalistic ideas are subtle and their interpretations often too daring for the average person, it is important to get a good grounding in the Bible and Jewish philosophy before engaging in the study of Jewish mysticism.

Recently, Jewish mysticism has been attracting a growing number of Hollywood celebrities and stars in search of spiritual fulfillment and insights into the relationship between God and humans. One of the most popular star seekers is none other than Madonna, who is said to have studied kabbalah during her pregnancy in order to find out which would be the best day on which to have her child delivered. Kabbalah centers continue to attract celebrities, both Jewish and non-Jewish. Among the reputed disciples are Courtney Love, Barbra Streisand, Elizabeth Taylor, and Roseanne Barr, just to name a few.

10. Jewish Renewal

The term Jewish Renewal refers to an informal movement of organizations and individuals dedicated to reclaiming the Jewish people's sacred purpose of partnership with the divine in the inseparable task of healing the world. Jewish Renewal groups seek to bring creativity, relevance, joy, and an all-embracing awareness to spiritual practice as a path to healing one's body and mind.

The current phenomenon of Jewish Renewal traces its roots to the havurah movement, feminism, and other late-twentieth-century phenomena, but primarily to the work of Shlomo Carlebach and Zalman Schachter Shalomi. Both of these charismatic rabbis were trained in the Lubavitch Hasidic movement but later left it to found their own institutions and plant the seeds of renewal worldwide. ALEPH: Alliance for Jewish Renewal grew out of the B'nai Or Religious Fellowship founded by Reb Zalman in 1962.

Many Jewish Renewal groups put their emphasis on direct spiritual experience and kabbalistic teaching. They are known for their creative liturgy and often use meditation, dance, and chant. There is a large, worldwide network of Jewish Renewal communities.

Jewish Renewal is not "New Age" Judaism, although it is often referred to by that name. Jewish Renewal uses age-old techniques (meditation, chant, dance) that have been present in Judaism throughout the ages. Because these techniques have been lost for so long thanks to assimilation, many contemporary Jews simply are unaware of them. That is one reason why so many spiritually sensitive Jews have sought spiritual expression in other faith traditions, such as Buddhism.

11. L'chayim, when raising a glass to make a toast

L'chayim is a Hebrew word meaning "To life." According to an incident described in the Talmud, the custom of toasting with the word l'chayim was originated by the great scholar Akiba. At a banquet he gave in honor of his colleague Shimon, he is said to have offered each guest a glass of wine and to have saluted them with the words "To the life and health of the rabbis and their disciples" (Talmud, Shabbat 67b).

CHAPTER **12**

Keeping Kosher
and Jewish Foods

1. The keeping kosher and health connection

Some people claim that that the fish and seafood forbidden by Jewish law yield a higher level of cholesterol than kosher fish. Although this may be, the Torah is clearly unconcerned with the hazards of too much cholesterol. In reality, there is no evidence that kosher eating is necessarily a healthier diet than nonkosher.

With the exception of holiness, the Torah does not present a rationale for the laws of keeping kosher. The most common misconception about the kosher regulations is that they are an ancient health measure that may have had a place in antiquity, but, what with modern methods of slaughtering, regular government inspection, and sanitary food preparation, are now an anachronism that should be discarded. Of course, one should not overlook concern for disease and the attempt to achieve purity in the kosher laws. However, if Jews have derived any health benefits from the dietary laws (such as lower incidence of trichinosis, which can be traced to eating pork), they have been unexpected.

2. What glatt kosher really means

The word glatt in Yiddish means "smooth." As a technical term in the dietary laws, it means that the lungs of a slaughtered animal were perfectly smooth with no lesions of any kind. Meat from such animals is preferred by certain extremely punctilious Jews, but in fact meat from animals with scarred lungs is also kosher.

Many people erroneously think that glatt kosher means "extra kosher" or a higher standard of kosher. As a result, purveyors of many foods other than meat, such as poultry, fish, candy, and even dairy, label their products as glatt kosher in order to get more customers. It is technically inaccurate and misleading to do this, since glatt specifically relates to meat.

3. Kosher labeling of food

Various organizations, generally in cooperation with well-trained Orthodox rabbis, supervise the manufacture and processing of kosher foods. A company wishing to have its food certified kosher must apply to one of these organizations. They carefully investigate the manufacturing techniques and ingredients to determine whether they meet the kosher standards of the certifying organization. There are currently more than ten thousand food products certified kosher by these organizations.

More than a hundred organizations nationwide offer rabbinic certification, and each has its own distinct symbol that appears on the food product. One of the most popular and largest is the Union of Orthodox Congregations, which certifies thousands of products manufactured by more than one thousand firms. The Union is known as the OU, and its symbol is a letter U with a circle around it. One of the smallest kashrut certifiers is an individual rabbi in Pittsburgh who certifies a brand of soft drink.

Some kosher products simply carry the letter K on their packages, to indicate that they are under rabbinic supervision but not necessarily Orthodox supervision. The name of the certifying agent can be determined by writing or e-mailing the manufacturer directly.

4. The ideal Jewish diet

The ideal Jewish diet is vegetarian. After all, according to the Torah, it was only after the Flood that human beings were first permitted to eat meat. Adam and Eve, in the ideal life of the Garden of Eden, were only permitted the produce of fruit trees as food to be eaten. However, the advent of the dietary laws of keeping kosher created a good working compromise, allowing Jews to eat animal flesh while establishing limits that spare the animal undue pain and at the same time refine our sense of compassion.

In recent years, some environmentally conscious Jews have been supplementing the Torah laws of kashrut. For example, along with just avoiding non-kosher food, such as ham and shellfish, they buy neither tomatoes treated with pesticides nor ecologically harmful cleaning products.

In the United States, factory farming has become a popular method of choice for raising animals, both kosher and non-kosher ones. The animals are often kept in cramped, quite despicable conditions. In the case of veal, which comes from a calf and is kosher, the problem is extreme. To ensure the tenderness of the meat, factory-farmed calves are immobilized in a contraption that does not permit them to graze. Instead, the head is positioned over a trough so that the animal can be force-fed until its final days. There are Jews today who choose to refrain from eating any kind of meat when they know that the animal from which the meat is derived was treated without true concern for its welfare.

Jews who consider eating veal to be treif (unkosher) and who will not buy vegetables treated with pesticides are known as eco-kosher. The concept of eco-kosher mandates living and consuming in accordance with the spirit of Jewish law.

As the greening of Judaism takes root across the country, eco-kosher is just one of many earth-friendly trends gaining momentum. Synagogues of all denominations are beginning to look for more ways to integrate ideas coming from the eco-kosher movement.

5. No sirloin steak for Jews who keep kosher

According to Ed Greenstein's essay on the dietary laws in the Eytz Chayim Torah and Commentary, the symbolic significance of the eating rules is most evident in the Torah's ban on eating the thigh muscle, or tendon, or nerve that was injured in Jacob's struggle with the divine being (Genesis 32:33). Because all of Jacob's immediate descendants are called literally "those issuing from his thigh" (a euphemism for his genitals), the ban draws attention to the ongoing condition of Israel as a people impaired by surviving. Dr. Greenstein posits that the impaired thigh tendon signifies the people Israel. And because of that symbolism, the Israelites are not to eat the part of the animal with which they are taught to identify themselves. Thus the eating rule is meant to remind Jews of who they are and from whom they are descended.

Interestingly, in some communities outside the United States, specially trained butchers take the trouble to remove all the veins, arteries, and forbidden fat from the hindquarters of an animal, thus making it kosher. This is tedious work, and most butchers are neither capable nor desirous of executing it.

6. Bread, the most important Jewish food

In Jewish tradition, no food is more important than bread. Proof of this can be adduced from Deuteronomy 8:8, in which bread (or, to be more specific, wheat, from which most bread is made) is mentioned before all other foods. It is for this reason that when the blessing over bread (ha-motzi) is recited at the beginning of a meal, it covers all the foods to be eaten during the course of the meal. Individual blessings need not be recited over the other foods unless they are not considered integral to the meal—such as grapes, dates, and other fruits.

Many passages throughout the Bible indicate the significance of bread. Whenever a guest is invited for a meal, bread is served (Genesis 18:5). In fact, so highly regarded is bread in Jewish tradition that the Talmud makes this statement: "Four things have been said in connection with bread: raw meat should not be placed on it [meat might spoil the bread]; a full cup of wine should not be passed over it [some wine might spill on the bread]; it should not be thrown around; it should not be used as a prop for a dish" (Berachot 50b).

7. Aversion to swine flesh

The special aversion of Jews to the flesh of the pig goes back to the Hasmonean period (second century b.c.e.), when the Syrian Greeks, who had occupied Palestine, tried to force Jews to sacrifice pigs in the Temple and eat their flesh. The Talmud says: "Cursed is the one who raises pigs."

8. Winged swarming things

"Locusts of every variety, crickets of every variety, and grasshoppers of every variety" are considered kosher according to Leviticus 11:22, but the rabbis have generally disapproved their use. It is interesting to note that the Jews of Rabat and other communities in Morocco do eat grasshoppers (chagavim).

9. Superkosher Milk

Many Orthodox Jews use only milk that has been under careful surveillance by a Jew from the moment of milking to the time of bottling. Such close supervision offers assurance that at no time during processing was the milk of a non-kosher animal or some other prohibited ingredient mixed in with it. Milk carefully guarded in this manner is called chalav Yisra'el ("milk of Israel").

10. Pâté de foie gras

Geese are force-fed to fatten them, thus enlarging their livers. From such oversized comes the delicacy known as pâté de foie gras (goose liver paste). Religious authorities are divided about the propriety of using such livers, since force-feeding is painful to animals and Jewish law prohibits inflicting pain on living creatures. The chief rabbi of Israel ruled that force-feeding is permissible because the pain inflicted is negligible and the economic gain considerable.

11. Waiting period between eating meat and dairy

Since the taste of meat stays on the palate for a while, a waiting period is required by Jewish law before eating dairy foods. The precise interval is not specified in the Talmud, and one therefore finds considerable variations from community to community. The length of the waiting period often depends on the type of meat eaten.

The waiting time after eating a meat product and before eating a dairy food can extend from one to six hours. After eating meat, Orthodox Jews who have their roots in Holland wait one hour. German Jews wait three hours, and East European and most Sephardic Jews wait a full six hours. The same waiting applies to the eating of dairy foods after eating fowl.

With regard to the wait between dairy and meat, most rabbinic authorities call for a period of at least thirty minutes from the time one eats soft cheese and other dairy products to the time one consumes meat. Hard cheeses, unlike soft varieties, cling to one's teeth and palate, and some strict authorities require that one wait a full six hours before consuming meat products.

12. Non-kosher wine

Talmudic law states that wine used in connection with idol worship is forbidden to Jews, as is wine touched by idolaters. The prohibition was extended by the rabbis to include wine made by non-Jews even if never intended for idolatrous purposes, and that ban has been carried over to this day, despite the fact that there are no longer idolaters in our midst. According to the Orthodox rabbinate, wine handled by non-Jews, known in Hebrew as yeyn nesech, may not be consumed.

For the most part, wine making in the United States is automated from the time grapes are fed into vats until the wine appears in sealed bottles. Based on the fact that no person has contact with the wine during the automated process, some rabbis have ruled that wines manufactured in this manner in the United States are kosher, although others have expressed concern about the use of so-called fixing agents of non-kosher origin.

Since wine that had been boiled was not permitted in pagan worship, Jewish law regards wine that has been boiled as kosher because it cannot be associated with pagan use.

Many producers of kosher wines boil their wine after the pressing stage. Such wine is considered kosher regardless of who has processed it. The words yayin mevushshal ("boiled wine") often appear on bottles of kosher wine so processed.

13. Jewish food recommendations

The Jerusalem Talmud (Kiddushin 4:12) says that "one should not live in a city that does not have a vegetable garden." The diet of most Jews in past centuries was primarily vegetarian, meat being eaten only on the Sabbath, holidays, and festive occasions.

For a wholesome diet, the scholar Maimonides, in his Sefer Refu'ot ("Book of Health"), recommends bread baked from flour that is neither too old nor too fine. He also recommends cheese, butter, white-meated fish with firm flesh, goat and sheep meat, and chicken. He considers fresh fruits to be unwholesome, but recommends dried fruits and wine.

Olives were extremely popular in talmudic times, although white olives, it was believed, affected the memory. Olive oil was recommended for old men—as the aphorism puts it, "Bread for young men, oil for old men, and honey for children."

Radishes were said to be good for one's health, but onions were to be avoided because of their pungent odor.

Finally, the Talmud suggests that the following foods have a positive effect on sexual potency: eggs, fish, garlic, wine, milk, cheese, and fatty meats (Berachot 40a, Sotah 11b, Yoma 18a). On the other hand, salt and egg barley were said to diminish potency. Ezra the Scribe decreed that garlic was to be eaten on Friday nights because "it promotes and arouses sexual desire."

14. Never mix fish and meat

In talmudic times, Jews believed that eating fish together with meat was unhealthy, and specifically that it caused leprosy. For that reason the rabbis forbade the cooking of meat and fish together in the same pot and the serving of fish and meat on the same plate. (Talmud, Pesachim 76b) The Code of Jewish Law also warns against eating fish and meat together, considering it harmful to one's health (Yoreh Deah 116:2). Moses Isserles, in his Notes, adds: "One should also not roast the two together because the fragrance of one penetrates the other, but if it was done inadvertently the food may be eaten." The paragraph that follows in the code does not require a waiting period between the eating of meat and the eating of fish, but does suggest that rinsing the mouth or chewing on something hard, such as bread, after eating meat to help dislodge any food particles trapped in the teeth.

In many traditional Jewish homes, soup (usually chicken soup) is served between the fish and meat courses at Sabbath and holiday meals. The original reason for serving soup was probably to cleanse the palate.

15. Bee honey in Jewish tradition

The Torah (Leviticus 11:20–23) indicates that most insects are not kosher. Certain kinds of locusts and crickets are exceptions. The bee is not listed as kosher, and yet the honey that comes from it is. The Talmud posits that honey is kosher even though it comes from a non-kosher insect because the bee itself does not produce the honey. It merely stores the honey in its body while carrying it from flower to flower to the beehive. Of course it is now known that during the time the nectar is being carried by the worker bee to the beehive, a chemical reaction takes place in which the nectar is converted into a sweet, thick liquid.

Honey derived from fruits (dates, figs, grapes, carob) is mentioned often in the Torah. Deuteronomy 8:8 lists honey as one of the seven foods with which the Land of Israel is blessed. To render "a sweet savor on the altar," honey was brought by the Temple priests as an offering of first fruits. (Leviticus 2:12). The Talmud (Berachot 44b) speaks of honey as one of the seven healing substances. Bee honey became a favorite Rosh Hashanah food, for on that holiday Jews greet each other with words that express hope for a good and sweet year. Thus the custom of dipping an apple into honey on the eve of Rosh Hashanah.

16. The Pomegranate: A Favorite Jewish Symbol

Along with figs and grapes, pomegranates were favored in Bible times. The pomegranate was one of the foods that the scouts sent out by Moses (Numbers 13:23) brought back with them from Canaan as proof that the Promised Land was fertile. The pomegranate was identified with fertility because of its many seeds. Some students of Jewish law claim that a pomegranate has 613 seeds, hence its identification with the 613 commandments Jews are obliged to observe.

Because of its popularity, the pomegranate has been widely used as a symbol in Jewish art. The two pillars of the First Temple (I Kings 7:18) were ornamented with pomegranate representations. Pomegranates were also embroidered on a garments of the high priest. (Exodus 28:33).

In more recent times ark curtains have often been decorated with embroidered representations of pomegranates. The pomegranate's shape inspired the design of the crowns placed on the two finials of a Torah scroll. These crowns are called rimmonim (Hebrew for "pomegranates").

17. Salt on the table

Notable on the Jewish table at mealtimes in traditional settings is the presence and use of salt. Like water for washing the hands, salt is an integral part of the table setting. The reasons given for the presence of salt date back to both biblical and talmudic times. In the time of the Temple, salt was used with all the sacrifices brought to the altar. Insofar as the Temple is no longer in existence, Jewish tradition posits that a person's table is likened to an altar. Thus, when a Jew makes a blessing over bread, salt is added as a symbolical sacrificial act. Here are some additional reasons for having salt on the table and using it ceremonially:

> The relationship between sprinkling salt on one's bread and eating aligns with the Bible phrase "by the sweat of your brow shall you get bread."
> The Torah notes that Joseph invited his brothers to a meal of bread and salt.
> Salt reminds us of the sin offerings offered in the Temple. The Hebrew word machal, "forgive," has the same three letters as the word for salt, "melach."
> Salt is common and inexpensive. When living in luxury, people should give thought to the more stringent and austere ways of living and remember that food is a divine gift.

Bringing salt and bread to a house as welcoming gifts for new occupants is an old custom. One researcher on ancient Jewish customs explains that bringing bread and salt into a new home before moving in is symbolic of the hope that food may never be lacking in that home.

18. Eating Right

A rabbi in suburban Minneapolis–St. Paul, Morris Allen, has organized a movement to create a new form of kosher certification which he calls hechsher tzedek ("justice seal"). As the name implies, this certification would be given only to food companies committed to justice in food preparation as well as to the laws of kashrut. Put another way, the hechsher tzedek puts the treatment of human beings at least on par with the treatment of animals.

To earn the hechsher tzedek certification, an employer would have to pay wages consistent with regional rates, provide employees with adequate health care and vacation benefits, and offer safety training to workers in a language they understand, among other requirements. The hechsher tzedek certification would augment, rather than replace, existing certifications, most of them issued by Orthodox councils in America.

19. GPS Goes Glatt

Global positioning system satellites may have an eye on nearly everything on the planet, but what they cannot see is a restaurant's kosher certification. Yitzie Katz, a resident of Queens, New York, has closed this information gap by mapping more than a thousand restaurants and founding a website where his list can be downloaded, www.KosherRestaurantsGps.com. More than four hundred users have downloaded the $18 list, which includes the phone numbers and addresses of the restaurants, as well as a reminder to call the restaurant in order to verify the kosher certification. In addition to kosher restaurants, Mr. Katz has included in the data base a listing of over two thousand minyanim (prayer groups) across the United States and Canada. Currently he is working on a list of mikvehs (ritual baths) and a way to put the database of kosher restaurants on his website for the convenience of travelers.

CHAPTER 13

The Jewish Woman

1. Women, slaves, and minors

The ancient rabbis classified women as on par with slaves and minors in that none of these three categories, unlike men, is obligated to fulfill all of the 613 commandments. According to the Talmud, women are exempt from reciting the Shema and from putting on tefillin, but they are not exempt from reciting the Amidah prayer, placing a mezuzah on the doors of their homes, or saying the blessing (grace) after meals.

Another probable reason for binding women with slaves and minors (under the age of thirteen) is that the members of these three categories were not totally independent persons. Women were tied to their husbands in marriage and in a sense were their property. Slaves owed total allegiance to their masters. And minors, of course, were under the control of their parents.

2. America's First Bat Mitzvah.

America's first Bat Mitzvah was Judith Kaplan Eisenstein, daughter of Rabbi Mordecai Kaplan, the founder of the Reconstructionist movement. Her Bat Mitzvah took place in Philadelphia in the year 1922. This event led the way for so many young women today having their Bat Mitzvah ceremony as a legitimate religious life-cycle event.

3. Women and Jewish prayer

According to traditional Jewish law, women are required to observe all of the negative commandments in the Torah. These are the commandments that begin with the words "You shall not." However, women are exempt from some of the positive commandments. The Talmud (Mishnah Kiddushin 1:7) ruled that women are not obligated to observe positive commandments that are dependent upon time (i.e., commandments that must be observed at a specific time of day or year.)

This law was enacted to free women of obligations that they would be unable to meet without hardship. For instance, for women to recite prayers in the morning when they are preoccupied with their homes and children would be unduly difficult. Hence, the rabbis ruled that women, unlike men, are not obligated to recite all the prayers, although they are free to do so if they wish.

There is no unanimity of opinion among the rabbis of the Talmud or later scholars as to which positive time-bound commandments women are not obligated to observe. Generally, however, the view of Maimonides is accepted. He lists in his Book of Mitzvot the following commandments from which women are exempt: recital of the Shema, wearing tefillin, counting the Omer, living in a sukkah, reciting the lulav and etrog prayers, and listening to the blasts of the shofar.

Interestingly, women are obligated to light the hanukkiah on Hanukkah even though this is a time-related positive commandment and therefore one would expect women to be exempted. The reason for this is that women as well as men witnessed the miracle of Hanukkah. The lighting of Hanukkah candles is only one of several time-bound positive mitzvot from which the early talmudic scholars exempted women but which later rabbis considered mandatory. Among them are reciting Kiddush on the Sabbath, fasting on Yom Kippur, eating matzah on Passover and celebrating festivals, hearing the Scroll of Esther on Purim, and drinking four cups of wine on Passover.

4. "Thank you for not making me a woman"

The traditional morning service includes fifteen morning blessings, one of which says: "Praised are You, Adonai our God, for not making me a woman." Over the centuries this blessing has been understood as an expression of thanks by men for the good fortune of having been born male and thus privileged to perform so many more commandments than a woman. Women, in contrast, simply thank God for having made them in accordance with God's will. Today, many prayerbooks in the more liberal branches of Judaism use the latter formulation for both genders, so that both men and women offer thanks for being made according to God's will.

5. Separation of the Sexes

In Orthodox synagogues, men and women are seated in separate sections of the sanctuary, marked off by a divider called a mechitzah, in order not to subject men to sexual distraction or temptation. The tradition of separating the sexes is also followed at weddings and other social gatherings even when not held in a synagogue. At some Orthodox weddings held in hotels or catering halls, men and women are generally seated on opposite sides of the room.

Many Hasidic sects go much further, requiring that men and women be seated separately even at the festive meal following the wedding ceremony. A movable partition is stretched down the center of the hall, and men eat and dance between courses on their side of the divider, while the women do the same on their side of the room.

6. Prohibition of women serving as witnesses

The Talmud (Mishnah Shevuot 4:1) states that "an oath of testimony applies to men but not to women." This refers to the biblical law (Leviticus 5:1) that a man who can offer testimony but refuses must bring a sin offering. The question is asked in the Talmud (Shevuot 30a:): "How do we know that women are ineligible as witnesses?" And the answer is that the verse in Deuteronomy 19:17 referring to witnesses says, "And the two men shall stand;" thus we know that witnesses must be men.

Maimonides, in his Mishneh Torah, comments that when the Torah refers to witnesses, it uses the masculine form, implying that it is only men who can serve as witnesses. Joseph Caro in the Code of Jewish Law disagrees, pointing out that often, when the Torah uses the masculine form, it is really referring to both sexes.

Some scholars believe that Jewish law prohibits women from serving as witnesses and offering testimony because in most cases in talmudic times women owned no property and were supported totally by their husbands. Therefore, if a woman had been allowed to testify and her testimony proved inaccurate, damages could not be collected from her, as would be done in the case of a man who gave incorrect testimony.

It is worth noting that in talmudic and later times women were called upon as witnesses in matters in which they were particularly knowledgeable, such as women's purity (e.g., the menstrual laws), and in cases where a husband was missing and only a woman was available to offer testimony.

In the more liberal branches of Judaism, women have full equality and can serve as reliable witnesses.

7. What does "Be fruitful and multiply" really mean?

How many children must one have in order to comply with the Torah's commandment "Be fruitful and multiply" (Genesis 1:28)? This was discussed centuries ago in the Talmud by the schools of Hillel and Shammai, two leading schools of interpretation at the time. Hillel and his followers posited that a married couple must have one boy and one girl in order to satisfy the commandment. The school of Shammai contended that it was necessary to have two boys (Talmud, Yevamot 61b).

The Hillel school based its view on the verse in the Torah, "And God created man in his own image . . . male and female created He them" (Genesis 1:27). This verse, they asserted, emphasizes the equality of the sexes as perceived by God. The school of Shammai held that since Moses had two sons and no daughters, and he was the greatest of the prophets, having two sons should be seen as satisfying the biblical command.

Generally the opinion of the Hillel school is followed, and rabbinic authorities are quite unanimous in considering that one has fulfilled his religious obligation if his family consists of not fewer than one son and one daughter!

8. Can a woman be a mohel?

There are many Jewish rituals that women do not practice even though they are legally permitted to do so. For instance, although Jewish law in theory allows a woman to act as a ritual slaughterer (shochet), this is traditionally a male occupation and women are discouraged from entering it.

The same is true of circumcision. Jewish law does permit a woman to be a mohel and perform ritual circumcisions. Tzipora, the wife of Moses, circumcised her son. Today there are some females in the United States who perform ritual circumcisions, but the profession of mohel continues to be dominated by men.

9. Healing prayers in the name of the mother

In Judaism, a person is traditionally identified by his or her father's name, in the form so-and-so son of [father's name] or so-and-so daughter of [father's name]. This is how an individual is identified when called up to the Torah and how the names of the bride and groom are written in the marriage contract of traditional Jews. During a time of illness, however, when a prayer for healing is recited, a different form of identification used. The ill person is referred to as so-and-so son [daughter] of [mother's name].

Using the mother's name during an illness was already in vogue in talmudic times. The scholar Abaye said, "My mother told me that all prayers for recovery must contain the name of the mother" (Talmud, Berachot 24a). Presumably this is because mothers are viewed as more compassionate than fathers, and therefore a prayer in the mother's name is more likely to elicit a merciful response. The Zohar, commenting on the Torah portion of Lech Lecha (Genesis 12–17), makes a similar point when it says that all appeals to supernatural beings must be made in the name of the mother.

CHAPTER **14**

Jewish Expressions

1. "From your mouth to God's ears"

The wonderful Jewish expression "From your mouth to God's ears" implores that somehow a beneficial occurrence should find its way from the earthly realm of the person's words to the compassionate ears of God in heaven so that God can activate the words. The Yiddish for this expression is foon diyn mohl tzu Gott's ehvrn. The expression has probably been uttered by every Jewish mother who ever spoke Yiddish and wanted to be sure that God was brought into the conversation.

2. "God Forbid"

Both the Hebrew language and Yiddish have the expression "God forbid" in their vocabulary. In Hebrew, the phrase is chas v'shalom ("pity and peace"), and in Yiddish, nitdawgehdacht, which literally means "it shouldn't happen here." These common Jewish expressions are used as a prophylactic: "Be careful you don't hurt yourself, chas v'shalom."

3. Yiddishe kawp

The term yiddishe kawp (literally "a Jewish head") is used to refer to someone who is clever, shrewd, cunning, bright, and alert. A person with a so-called "Jewish head" can immediately grasp a difficult situation, understand and resolve a dilemma, and the like. Having a yiddishe kawp is not restricted to being Jewish. Many a non-Jewish person can be admired for having a yiddishe kawp.

4. "It was truly bashert"

Bashert is a popular Yiddish expression that means "destined" or "meant to be." It can be used as a term of resignation, confirmation, uncertainty, hesitation, or expectation. When a traditional Jew finds his or her mate and marries that person, a Yiddish-speaking family member is very likely to say that the marriage was indeed bashert—destined to be.

5. Mazal tov

Traces of the ancient Jewish belief that the stars hold an influence over people can be found in several expressions used by the ancient rabbis. The most familiar one is the expression mazal tov, which is often today interpreted to mean "good luck" or "good fortune." It actually refers to "a good star." A mazal in Hebrew is a constellation of stars. An unfortunate fellow today is still called a shlimazel—one who has no mazal, one on whom fortune does not smile.

In several talmudic passages it is stated that every one of us has a celestial body (mazal), a particular star which is our patron from conception and from birth, and which perceives things unknown us. The talmudic tractate of Nedarim 39b describes the phenomenon of two persons born under the same star as sharing both a bodily and spiritual kinship.

The Hebrew term siman tov is essentially the same as mazal tov, although it literally translates as "good omen." The two expressions are used either together or separately for everything from getting a good grade on an exam to buying a new home.

6. "Until one hundred and twenty"

"Until one hundred and twenty" is a common expression evoking hopes for a healthy and long life. It is used when talking to or about someone, and is always used in a positive way. The phrase derives from the Torah's statement on the death of Moses: "And Moses was a hundred and twenty years old when he died. His eye was not dim, nor his natural force abated" (Deuteronomy 34:7).

In Hebrew the phrase is ad meyah v'esreem shanah. In Yiddish you might hear biz ah hoondred un tzveahntzik yohrn.

7. Yasher koach

Following an aliyah to the Torah, or the opening or closing of the holy ark, the honoree may be traditionally congratulated with the Hebrew phrase yasher koach on returning to his or her seat. The truest pronunciation of the term is yisher ko'checha, meaning "may you grow in strength." Sephardic Jews often use the term chazak u'varuch ("may you be strong and blessed") as a congratulatory phrase to a person who has had a ritual honor.

8. Gezunterheit

Gezunterheit is a Yiddish expression with several meanings. It usually means "in good health," emphatically, reinforcing something positive or giving hearty approval. However, it can also be turned around and used in a sarcastic fashion.

9. Mensch

In English, "he's a real man" generally connotes a macho male, one who has numerous romantic liaisons. The Yiddish word mensch ("man") implies something very different. A mensch is a decent, honest, reliable, trustworthy person. It is not gender-based, and thus a woman too can be referred to as a mensch.

The term mensch is used in a variety of contexts. "Be a mensch" might be the advice given to a person who is not treating another person fairly. The related word menschlikh-keit refers to ethical behavior in general. "The important thing," one might say, "is to act with menschlikhkeit."

10. Tzaddik

Tzaddik is the Hebrew word for a righteous person, but when Jews use the word today, as in "She's a real tzaddik," they usually mean "saint.' Thus a person who is referred to as a tzaddik is an extremely kind and righteous person with saintly powers and great faith. In the Hasidic movement, the term denotes the movement's rabbinic leader.